Forged in Fire

50 Fight-to-Win Tactics to Help Your Business Succeed

TIM STOUT

DEDICATION

To the love of my life, Christy, thank you for always believing in me and my crazy dreams.

ACKNOWLEDGMENTS

Thanks to my dad, Bob, for being my prime supporter and mentor.

To my mother, Carla, thanks for having in faith in me when no one else did, teaching me the love of reading and learning, and showing me what true love and compassion really are.

Thanks to my childhood best friend, Cliff, for always pointing me in the right direction.

To my first boxing coach, the late Marvin Fritts, thanks for teaching me the art of boxing and making me the fighter I am today.

To the late Cobb Riddle, a man of many talents, thanks for always seeking to bring out the best in me, inside and outside of the ring.

Thanks to Casey Oxendine for being a best friend, coach, manager, and mentor.

Thanks, Scott Martino, for saying "you should write a book" and believing in me even when I didn't.

Thanks to Ariel McCrory for bringing my stories and lessons alive with this book, I couldn't have done this without your help and persistence.

Thanks to my real estate team for forcing me to level up every day, I'm so proud to be in business with you. Thanks to my mentor and business coach, David Keesee, for challenging me and helping my dreams come true.

Finally, I'd like to thank everyone who lives in Mountain City, Tennessee for helping me and believing in this small-town boy.

Table of Contents

Introduction: From Here to There

Are you ready to learn fifty fight-to-win tactics that can change your life, guarantee your success, and forge your business through fire? This book will change your mindset so that you can get from here to beyond your ceiling of limitation. This book will reshape your business and help it obtain unthinkable wins in its market.

I'd like to share with you a brief background of how I started employing the fifty fight-to-win tactics in the following chapters to my life and business, which completely changed my mindset and life. No matter what kind of a season life brings, we can be successful if we change our mindset. When we change our mindset, we change our expectations and outcomes, and those outcomes change our lives.

A few years ago, finances were so tight that my wife sold her jewelry for us to buy groceries. I was training and fighting professionally, all the while hoping that our finances would add up to what we needed...but they were not. I needed to bring in more income. So I made up my mind to retire from my fighting career and transition into a new career altogether. I needed a career without a ceiling of limitations that would pay me for my hard work and discipline. A career that I could also be coached to improve my techniques since that's what I was used to in the fighting world.

I prayed about this decision but wasn't finding much clarity. A few days passed, and as I taught a class at the gym to a few successful ladies, I realized they lacked good work ethic and discipline that I believed was necessary for them to excel in both exercise and business. They both worked in sales and I figured that if I had more discipline than they did, then I should also work in sales.

When I told my wife about my idea, her response was:

"Are you sure? You can't sell anything."

But I had a feeling that if I strived to be the hardest worker in sales and increase my discipline, I could guarantee my success. "I don't have to sell; I just have to be the hardest worker in the room."

It is a good challenge to become the hardest worker in the room that you are in now, and then change rooms to a room of twice as many people where you are the *least* hardest worker so that you can be challenged to work even harder. As you self-educate yourself and become more disciplined, switch rooms again. Keep switching rooms as soon as you become the hardest worker in each room. There will always be bigger rooms for you to improve your behaviors, further your discipline, learn more efficient procedures, and keep pushing through to the next level. With discipline and hard work, you will automatically surpass a large majority of other folks on the road to success.

My wife and I borrowed the money needed for my real estate courses and license. We stretched our finances to make it happen. Soon I realized that I had a knack for selling houses and I loved helping people, but I needed more training. More coaching.

As a pro-athlete, everyone needs an excellent coach. No matter how good you think you are. Tiger Woods had a coach, Michael Jordan had a coach, and Mike Tyson had a coach. Behind every decent athlete there is a good coach. Behind every stellar athlete there is a stellar coach. I needed someone who could challenge me at a high level and open my eyes to strategies and systems that I couldn't think of on my own. Everyone needs a coach in their field of business, preferably one with the experience and wisdom needed to succeed. So I hired a coach. Not just any coach, but Coach David Keesee from the Keesee Company. Coach David is a stellar coach and the best decision I've ever made in my real estate career.

In my second year of real estate, I closed seventy-six transactions with very little assistance and without working past four o'clock in the afternoon, since I ran my Mixed Martial Arts gym in the afternoons. Real estate was unpredictable and subject to fluctuate with the changing housing market, so I needed a predictable source of alternative income. I worked six hours every night at the gym since that was a stable source of income and place of respite for me.

I realized that I could be successful at a high level in real estate with the right coaching and self-education, work ethic, and discipline. I read forty to sixty books a year to further my education and expand my way of thinking to lead to self-growth.

We each control our self-education and self-growth, so it is up to *us* (and no one else) to discipline ourselves to make these areas great.

I hired an assistant for my real estate business and sold the majority share of the MMA gym to a longtime friend and training partner. I learned through coaching how to properly manage my time, and while selling real estate was the highest and best use of my time, running the MMA gym was the highest and best use of his time.

As a small team working full time, we closed 126 transactions. I spent more time investing in the real estate career and building the team by hiring buyer's agents, listing agents, client care managers, listing managers, transaction coordinators, and the like.

Each hire had to be coachable with a high work ethic and hold the same moral beliefs as me and the other team members. Since I hire people with the same mindset as me and the rest of the team, we have an extremely low turnover rate since everyone is on board with the same mission and vision for the team.

I researched how to make my team stronger and more efficient, listened to books, went to seminars, took classes, and was coached to obtain the best advice I could in leading a team well. Growing the team was so exciting as we challenged ourselves to push forward to meet our goals. I enjoyed giving the team all the credit for our success, they are the rock stars of the business and deserve all the praise for their hard work and discipline.

The next year with a determined mindset and growth of the team, we closed 200 transactions. This ranked us as the top sales team in the area with some of the first agents to gross $1 million GCI (gross commission income) in the region.

My goal for 2018 was to replace myself with a listing specialist so that I could manage the team full time. With this change, the Atlanta team closed over 260 transactions and increased its numbers by about $2 million GCI, and I expanded my real estate business to the Northeast Tennessee and Southwest Virginia area.

It was necessary to partner with the right people for the expansion team to work well. My long-time best friend sold real estate in that area and I had recently met a smaller real estate group licensed in both Tennessee and Virginia who had great potential. With their coachability, same moral beliefs, and high work ethic, the marriage worked nicely. We now have a licensed Admin and three agents on the team, and it continues to grow. I travel to the Northeast Tennessee area every month to support, motivate, and train this team.

No one should expand their business just for the sake of expanding, or that business will have a faulty foundation. It is vital to have the right people, equip them well, and lead them well. If you cannot do these three things, then you should not expand your business.

Both teams enact the fifty fight-to-win tactics taught in this book and are excelling in their growth and productivity. As you read this book, you will be challenged to rethink your current mindset and business systems that keep you from reaching your full potential. You'll figure out what your team needs to do to triple your productivity numbers and climb to the top of the market. **You will realize that with the right mindset of discipline, positivity, and coachability, your team can be disciplined to focus its time and energy on what matters for the business, clients, and community. With these fifty fighting tactics, your business will be forged through fire and unlock a new pathway to success**.... Let's get started!

Chapter 1 - Feed Your People First

My siblings and I used to eat soup beans every day for every meal. We always thought that our dad just really loved soup beans. Which was strange to us because no one just LOVES soup beans. As we got older, we realized that he could feed a whole family of seven with just soup beans for about $1. (If you're not from around the northeast Tennessee area, soup beans translate into bagged pinto beans cooked into a soup). Growing up in a family of seven, we lived in a three-bedroom, one bathroom, 900 square feet home, and by certain standards we were poor. We never did without, but we never had extra. Both of my parents worked hard and wanted to provide, but we had a big family and lived in a less-income producing, rural area of the country. We always wore hand-me-down clothing and our cupboards were never very full, but we made do with what we had.

My dad worked for a trucking company for a while and when he came home from long trips, we all drove an hour away to pick him up. It was a family tradition for us to go out to eat at a fast food chain restaurant after we picked him up, nowhere special, but it was special for us.

I remember Dad always said that he was never hungry when we got to the restaurant. He never ordered food for himself. He waited until we were all finished and then he ate the leftovers from our plates. He fed us, but he didn't have enough money to feed himself. He made sure everyone else was fed before he ate.

This is not only a good lesson in parenting but also a good business practice. **As a leader in your business or team, you must feed your people first. Give your team the business that you would normally receive. Make sure your team is well taken care of before you are**. If your team is not well fed, your team will dissipate and business will crumble. **You must, in humility, care for yourself last if you want to be a good leader.** Make sure your team and business are well fed with the business that you would typically get first, and this will ensure that your team will thrive, not just survive.

This will enhance trust in the relationship between you and your co-workers. They will see that you truly care about their well-being, business, and families.

Another aspect of this story that I would like to focus on can be summed up in this word: limitless. Like some of you, I grew up in a big family, small house, poor community, and with little money. Did these characteristics define my future? No, I did. If you are currently living in a trailer or a mansion, if you have a well-paying job or none at all, whether you are wealthy by certain standards or trapped in debt, who cares! **These circumstances do not define who you are, and they definitely do not limit your potential. You are limitless.**

You can have the ability to provide for yourself, your family, your community, and team members in your future business. You are limitless! **You set the limits for yourself and your future, nothing else does.**

Don't believe a lie that because of your socioeconomic status or current circumstance that you will not amount to anything. I guarantee that you've already amounted to something great but have blinded yourself to it out of self-pity or lack of confidence. Want to know a quick way to get over self-pity? Replace the lies you are telling yourself with truth. **Truth that you have limitless potential you've not yet allowed yourself to unlock. If you want to start a business, then start one! Do not wait for the "perfect" time, because it may never come and tomorrow may not either**.

If you want to walk down a path but aren't sure what the path looks like along the way so you stare down the path terrified of what may be ahead, just start walking. You will never know what lies ahead until you take the first step. You'll figure everything else out as you go, just take the first damn step. You'll find that you'll unlock your potential and gain more confidence along the way. **Feed yourself with the truth and potential that you have been holding back, then turn around and feed others who are also waiting to take their first step down their path.**

Need help in starting a business? Go door-knock one hundred homes until you find one other person who supports your idea and wants to help you. Make one hundred phone calls until you find a business that would allow you to shadow their staff or interview their workers to learn what you may need to do to get from point A to point B in your business. Read books, learn from others, plan, and set your mind to a big ass goal that will achieve the success (and more) that you've been hoping for. When you start a business, make sure you have the money to pay your workers appropriately and give them the business they need for themselves and their families.

Take care of those who take care of you. Take the first step to help others and in doing so, you'll also help yourself. Feed your team before you feed yourself, and you'll build loyal relationships and an unstoppable business.

Chapter 2 - Training to Your Own Rhythm

Coach Cook was one of the last kickboxing coaches I had the privilege of training with when I was still fighting. Unlike my other coaches, Coach Cook would not allow me to train while listening to music. His reasoning was that the faster and more upbeat the music, the faster and harder I trained. **The more rhythm in the music, the more rhythm in my training.** The slower rhythm in the music, the slower I moved. Music created a rhythm that was unnatural and inconsistent to who I needed to train myself to be in the ring. I needed to learn how to tune out other voices and background noises so that I could focus solely on my training.

The business application is simple. **Do not watch or listen to what other people are doing in their businesses. Do not allow their rhythm to alter what your business is doing.** Pay attention to what your team needs to do to attain its goals. **Create your own rhythm that keeps the business steady and motivated, independent of what other businesses are doing.** Tune out the voices and actions of other businesses. You will become so distracted worrying about how other businesses are running that you will fail to run your business correctly.

If you are mimicking what other people are doing or constantly comparing your business to others, then you are simply forwarding the other business's goal. You are training to their music and rhythm. **You may be failing to forward your own goal and may even be deaf to your own goal since you are listening to their music and adapting their rhythm.** Work to your own rhythm. Do not let other voices or businesses distract you. Tune them out. **Remember what your goal is for the team and business,**

then work together as one organism to develop a rhythm to accomplish that big ass goal.

When people try to train to your rhythm and copy your systems and procedures, let them. No one will be able to do exactly what your team is doing since others will not have the consistent routine, will-power habits and discipline that your team will be operating from when your business implements the tactics of this book to succeed.

When copy-cats start doing what you are doing, they have already forfeited the game. Now your business is aware that you have the upper hand in setting the pace for everyone else. **Copy-cats do not have confidence in themselves to create their own successful policies or systems, and they will never have the authentic entrepreneurial ambition to do so.** Let them copy you as you stay ahead of them. **Take pride in the fact that your rhythm is so loud that people want to steal its thunder.** Compete even harder with the copy-cats to remain a few years ahead of them in your systems, procedures, and marketing plan.

It does not matter if people know the ins and outs of how your business runs and what is implemented to make the business run the way it does. People can copy your marketing plan and try to figure out all your secrets, but at the end of the day if they do not have the drive that you do, they will not get very far.

Even if everyone else in the world is privy to how you are running your business and tries to copy your rhythm, all they will ever do is copy and not truly compete. **You will remain the maestro of the tune and will continue to grow because of the high drive dedicated to your ability to pave your way, train to your own rhythm, and block out everything else**. Not only will other businesses see this, but so will the customers.

Everyone will know that your business has set the standard and was the first, the best, and the only to do what you're doing. Keep working to make sure that customers do not forget that your business is the original. **Let everyone know that your business has the creativity, focus, and uncharted ambition to stay ahead, and no one in the world can steal that from you.**

Chapter 3 - Calculating Your Aggression

Baby poisonous snakes can be the deadliest since, unlike adult snakes who have learned to reserve their venom, babies have not yet learned how to control their poison. When baby poisonous snakes feel vulnerable, they bite their attacker hard and pump extra venom into the attacker which leaves no poison left in their reserves for any other prey or predator. They have not yet learned how to control their aggression.

A fierce fighter who does not know how to control his aggression or strength is not a good fighter. He will exert too much energy and never get anywhere.

As a fighter I had to be taught how to use aggression to my advantage. When I first started fighting, I knocked a lot of people out and had a lot of fun doing it. In my first four fights I knocked out the opponent in the first 30-40 seconds. Of those four fights, I won three because of my blind aggression. I went in for the kill every time. But this fiery aggression hurt my endgame because I gassed (got out of breath) too quickly since all I did was fight with no endurance or strategy to win. This was not a strong, sustainable plan for success. My only goal was to get shit done in the cage and use my brute force to win. After listening to my coach, my game improved and I learned to calculate and pace my aggression throughout the fight. But I needed more training to strategize and win more fights in the long run by calculating my aggression.

In business, you need to use aggression to your advantage, but never use it recklessly. I am a very aggressive business owner, but there is a big difference between aggression and *controlled* aggression. **You must be in control. You must be consistent in your training and growth so that you're always improving your end game.**

The foundation must be set for a house before anything else is built. The same is true in business. A strong foundation must be built before the business can succeed. As an entrepreneur or business leader, you must be in control and cannot aggressively build a business without building a firm foundation.

Strategically pace yourself for the win instead of pushing and shoving with brute force to get ahead. **You'll gas out too quickly and never end up with real success if you rely on brute force and aggression to get you anywhere in life. The base to your business should stand on controlled systems and procedures before anything else can be built**. Be proactive in any and every part of the business so that items are taken care of immediately and efficiently. Keep good training and coaching in place to continuously improve your game. Then when you need to be aggressive, you will be aggressive while remaining in control.

Pace yourself so that your energy and time do not burn out too quickly. There is a time to be aggressive in business, just like there is a time to be aggressive in the cage. **Most importantly, you must protect yourself and your business from gassing out too quickly because of uncontrolled aggression, haphazard systems, or inconsistent training.** Pace yourself to endure the long game and you'll have a strong, sustainable strategy for success.

Chapter 4 - Pick Up the Broom

The greatest leaders in history led others by setting a great example in word and deed for them to follow. The greatest pastors led their congregations by setting a great example in word and deed. The greatest parents led their children by setting a great example in word and deed.

This kind of leadership requires a depth of humility and willingness to show others what is required of them by doing it first. If something needs to be done, these leaders will do the task themselves, whether great or small, and set the high standard for others to follow.

I started working my very first job as a cashier at a fast food restaurant in Mountain City, Tennessee when I was a teenager. Even though it was boring as hell, it was a paying job. And I needed it. One day my dad came to the restaurant when it was super slow, and I didn't have anything else to do besides stand behind the cash register and lean on the counter.

As dad walked up to the counter, he looked disappointed and said, "Timmy, you don't ever need to be standin' around at work. There's always somethin' for you to do."

"Dad, I've done everything they told me to do. I'm already done with my duties."

"Then son, pick up a broom. If you need to sweep this place ten times a day for you to stay busy, then do it." I never understood the importance of my father's words to me until I was in a management role myself.

Once I got into a management position, I found that there is always time to produce more business. Anytime I feel like I am done, I am not. There are always more handshakes I can make, more phone calls I can make, more places I can contribute my time to helping my business grow. **Stay busy. Pick up the broom, show others how things should be done. Be the example.** This was a lesson that took twenty years for me to learn and I wish I had learned it sooner. **So many more employees will trust your leadership if you lead them by example in word and deed.** Choose not to make the same mistake I did by failing to heed my father's words sooner in my business. Pick up the broom as your team's leader and clean the place better, faster, and more efficiently than they do, for this is true leadership. Refuse to piss away time and always choose to work, even if you think you're done.

In everything my coach expected me to do in the fight world, he did first and better than I did. Employees should not just do what their managers say because the boss says so, but employees should do what their managers say because they have seen their managers do it, do it more, and do it better.

Set the example by word and deed. For you to be a successful manager or team leader, your team must see that you call more people than they do and can generate more business than they are. **They need to see you do the work that they have been expected to do. You need to do it more, faster, and more effective**. You set the pace for your team.

Chapter 5 - Duck Walking a Mile

My first boxing coach, the late Marvin Fritts, was also a police officer and seemed to be best friends with the whole town. Coach Fritz was an influential mentor for me in life as well as in fighting. Coach taught me many valuable lessons and unlike most valuable lessons where I didn't realize what they taught me until years down the road, his valuable lessons explained their meaning immediately to me and matured me in more ways than he intended.

Coach Fritz was preparing me for a few upcoming fights in Knoxville, and part of his training forced me to run five miles a day. I hated those runs. On one day in particular, I was fixing to run my daily five mile stretch in complete misery and frustration. I had zero motivation to run since it was cold outside, but since I knew that Coach Fritz most likely had eyes on me to make sure I completed the run, I started out regardless.

About three miles into my run, I passed an alleyway and noticed that it could be a potential shortcut. This shortcut would save me a full mile - a lot of ground for a five-mile run. I figured that there was no way for anyone to notice me taking the shortcut, and I had finished most of the way through the run after all.

I took the shortcut down the alleyway. This wonderful decision saved me about 20% of my run.

I met up with Coach Fritz after my run, and his first words were, "Well, that was quick, Pocket." He called me strange nicknames. I don't know how he knew, but I knew I was busted.

Coach was like my Dad, no one could pull anything over on him without him figuring it out first.

"Ok, hop in the car." Coach Fritz opened his car door and motioned for me to join him. He took me back to the alleyway where I cheated, and I knew whatever he was going to do to me was going to be one hundred times worse than the run itself.

Coach made me duck walk all the way back from the point where I had cheated to the point where I should have ended the run, which was about a mile. A duck walk, for those of you who have never experienced this level of hell, is a squatting position where your butt is almost touching the ground as your feet move a little bit at a time while staying in the squatted position. It is horrible to do this for any amount of time.

He walked with me the whole way. There was no resting. No stopping. No saying sorry. No talking at all. He made sure that each step was as low as I could go and that I would make it the whole mile without cheating. All I could do was duck walk and listen to him yell at me to squat lower.

This was one of the greatest lessons I have ever learned.

He took me back to the specific point where the decision was made, the point where I should have obeyed and stayed straight in my way. When he brought me back to the point where I had essentially decided to deceive him and then punished me there, he disciplined me in the way I needed it to fully grasp the importance of this lesson.

There are no shortcuts that should ever be taken in business, no cutting corners in life, no cheating in discipline, and no skirting the system. There is no easy way to the finish line. There is always someone else watching you, so be honest. Be true. **Let no one have a reason to doubt your honesty. Do not give the devil a foothold in your business, your life, or your family.** Protect your family, your life, and your business by deciding right now to keep the pathway straight. Follow it no matter what temptations come along. Be ethical and keep a solid and honest reputation.

The moment you start cutting corners or justifying your actions in taking shortcuts in systems or reporting, leadership, and life in general, your discipline will diminish and the devil on your shoulder will grow bigger and bigger. **Learn this lesson now before your business and your life go to hell in a handbasket and you are forced to pay a price much heavier than duck walking a mile.**

Like the Bible says, the path is narrow and the way is steep, and few choose to follow the narrow way. Yet many choose the wider, easier shortcut that will cost you later in life and business. **Choose the narrow, steeper, less traveled on path that demands you to remain honest, ethical, and trustworthy above all things.** Be the leader that others can trust to make the right decision financially and morally for the business. **The moment you allow people to doubt your integrity is the moment you will pay a much higher price than Coach Fritz made me pay.** Understand this. Live by this.

Do not compromise your integrity for anything, for if you do, then prepare for your family, business, reputation and more to greatly suffer.

Chapter 6 - Sometimes it Takes a Head Kick

About fifteen years ago I trained a fighter who became a very successful pro-fighter and more than that, my best friend and fellow real estate agent. We had come to the point in our training where I was teaching necessary sparring technique to win a fight.

It was the first day of advanced sparring, and as we trained he kept his left hand low, which was a poor defensive move. Keeping the left hand low fails to protect the face or head from an opponent's blow. He thought it was tactical, but I thought it was lazy. After telling him multiple time to keep his left hand up, I kicked him in the head and knocked him unconscious since his head was left unprotected. When he woke up, he understood why I had kicked him in the head. His left hand was low which had left his head unprotected, as I had told him multiple times.

We sparred again but he failed to correct the same issue. I kicked him in the head again and knocked him out a second time. As he came around, he realized that if he would have brought his left hand up to protect his head, he would quit getting hit in the head. This all happened a third time before he finally understood.

He heard me tell him many times to keep his left hand up, then he physically experienced the issue and knew that I was right, but he still failed to correct the issue. No matter how many times I told him the same thing or even showed him the same thing, he needed to come to the realization on his own. No matter how long it took him to grasp. **My lessons to him were not nearly as good as the one lesson he taught himself** after getting kicked in the head and knocked unconscious three times.

Sometimes people must come to the realization of issues on their own. Telling them repeatedly is a waste of time since it doesn't make sense to them. Showing them does not make sense to them. Even disciplining them to learn the hard way may not make sense to them. **The only lesson that will ring sound to them will be the one lesson that they teach themselves after they come to the realization on their own.** The only solution that they'll want to apply to their problem may be their own solution, not yours.

In the business world, you as the responsible leader must do more than merely tell or show your team members, other staff, vendors, or clients that they are wrong. Telling or showing them that they are wrong makes them wrong. No one likes to be wrong. When they become wrong, they will build a wall against you and immediately become defensive. As soon as they become defensive, it hinders any constructive conversation that could be shared with them. **Instead of merely telling or even showing someone how they are wrong, the situation needs to be approached differently.**

Talk about the situation together and ask questions about how that problem could be fixed. Then listen. Truly listen to what they have to say. **Then implement.**

The moment that person comes up with the solution on their own, they OWN the solution. They are now a part of the solution instead of the problem, and the solution is more likely to be carried out. They have come to the realization on their own – even if you ask questions to catapult them to the realization – now they have taught themselves a lesson stronger than any other lesson you could ever teach them.

Your team members and staff must be put in positions to teach themselves. Ask questions that will enable your team to come to the right conclusions on their own. **As their responsible leader, make the necessary choices to allow your team members and clients to come to their own conclusions - which you lead them to through asking the right questions - and allow them to become**

part of the solution, not the problem. This will take practice so start now. Start asking questions that help your team members introspectively arrive to the solutions that will help them solve their issues and teach themselves the one lesson that they will understand.

Chapter 7 - Teaching without Beating

As a Mixed Martial Arts fighter, I had a mindset that if someone could not lift heavier weights than I could, then they should not teach me how to lift. If someone could not out-wrestle me, then from my perspective, they should not teach me to wrestle. If someone could not submit me, they should not teach me Jiu Jitsu strategies. If someone could not out-box me, they should not teach me to box. Although this thought process hadn't gotten me very far in improving my skills, I sure thought it had.

I started shutting people out and disregarding their advice since they could not physically dominate me. (I believe all fighters – and teenage boys - go through this phase at one point or another.) I closed my ears to what others had to say and refused to learn from others who had a lower skill set than me in an area.

One of my boxing coaches was in his 60s and although he was physically limited, he alone had forgotten more than I will ever know about fighting. He could not physically dominate me. Yet I realized he was the master and had so much knowledge to share with me, so I listened to him. He could not physically dominate me, so his skill set in that area was lower than mine at that time. But he was still the boss and I knew it. I wanted to sit at his feet and learn all that I could from him.

I began to realize that I shouldn't keep disregarding the wisdom of others because I was hell-bent on being such a macho-man. I needed to learn from someone who could not physically dominate me but was still better than me in a specific expertise. **Coach helped me realize that everyone has something to offer. No matter the level of expertise you think you have, you can always afford to learn from someone else.**

The alpha male in me who thought that I couldn't learn from others reflected a short-sighted thought process which limited me more than I knew. **My pride cut short my ability to learn since I refused to listen to others who had knowledge to share.** I thought I knew more than them. **I judged them from their ability within a certain skill set and didn't think that listening to their different perspective could improve my critical thinking, strategy, problem solving, focus, stability, and the like.**

Everyone will teach you something different if you open your ears. Once you taste a little bit of success, then you will begin to shut your ears and open your mouth more. This is the first spiral in a detrimental course downhill. **You will learn less and speak more which is backwards.**

You may think that no one will be able to teach you something that you don't already know, but this creates a pride in you that will be almost impossible to break.

You are not the best in the world, and you need the advice and wisdom of others to improve your skill set, systems, products, service, and more. You have much more discipline and knowledge to learn from others. The moment you attempt to prove to others that you know more than they do by speaking more and listening less, your business will begin to crumble. **The foundation of the business and future growth of the business cannot solely depend on one person who is deaf to the advice and wisdom of others.**

Instead of speaking more, you should barely speak. **Focus on listening. Listen until your ears bleed.** The person you should fear the most is the quietest person since that person knows the most.

Every person teaches you something if you take the time to listen. You can learn what NOT to do from a situation gone wrong. You can learn from a client's complaint that one of your systems or products needs improvement. You can learn from your staff from their good ideas to grow the business. You can learn from a supervisor when he reaffirms or critiques what you're doing.

You will see self-growth in yourself as you listen to others because your pride will be broken, and you'll become a humbler person. Keep your ears open and your mouth shut. Do this and you are guaranteed to learn more. You will become more successful. Not only in your business, but also in your life.

Chapter 8 - Win the First Round

If a fighter wins the first round in the ring, he sets himself up with the confidence he needs to win the next round. If he loses the first round, then it takes him twice the strength and will-power to even believe that he can win the next round. If he can push himself to make the first punch and win the first round, the hard part is out of the way and it's easier for him to win the next round and ultimately the fight. When I fought professionally, if I didn't give the first punch or win the first round of a fight, then I was not in the right frame of mind (or body) to win the following rounds.

When full-time athletes schedule their workout regiments, they make sure that their hardest workout of the day is completed early in the morning when they're completely rested and mentally in the game, and then throughout the rest of their day they focus on specific training. These athletes have already taken the time to train their body to better prepare for whatever tomorrow's challenges may bring. The science behind this is simple. If we do first what we do NOT want to do but need to do, then the rest of the day is wide open for doing the things that we want to do.

If athletes fail to complete the most difficult portion at the beginning of their day, they will not be in the right frame of mind or body to complete specific training later in the day, and it will take them twice as long to complete. The same ideology applies to business.

Engaging will-power and determination to do first in your day what you don't think you can do, or don't want to do, is one of the most important lessons you can learn in business. If you don't have habits in place to kick-start your day to a "win" in the mornings, a "win" over something you may not want to do or don't think you can do, then you will inevitably have less will-power, determination, and strength to do everything else you need to do in your day. **The morning is your time to win the first round.** Business leaders must live this lesson out every day to be successful.

The first moments when you wake up in the morning determine whether you will have a productive day or lazy day. Do you often decide to hit the snooze button when you first wake up? Schedule three alarms since you know you'll snooze all of them before you get up? **If you start the day by hitting the snooze button, you're already allowing yourself wiggle-room with your discipline and will continue to procrastinate what must be done throughout the day.** Since we interrupt our sleep cycles when we hit the snooze button, we interrupt our energy levels for the rest of the day.

If you get up when your first alarm rings and start your workout, read your Bible, have breakfast with your family, review your calendar for the day and prepare for its events, and do whatever else needs to be done before you go to work, then you are starting your day with the discipline needed to succeed. You are winning the first round. You are owning your morning.

When you start your morning with a "win," then you'll carry this mindset into your business dealings. You'll find yourself completing what you may not want to do first to get it out of the way to ensure that the rest of the day will be free from procrastination, and full of healthy income-producing activities for your business.

If you're in a management position where you must generate your own business and build your client base, like in real estate or another entrepreneurial position, then you wake up every morning unemployed and you must find your next employer. There is no motivator quite like unemployment. The morning is the only time that you can truly control what you do and set the pace for the rest of your day. Will you seek out business and be a "go-getter?" Or will you expect business to fall into your lap and then procrastinate in doing the items required to keep the little business you have now? Win the first round and take control of your morning, implementing the will-power habit to do what you may not want to do first so that you can have the strength and confidence needed to finish the day well.

Create a strict morning routine that will keep you on track for a productive day. Will you schedule a visit to the gym in the morning? You may know that if you wait until the evening, you'll either talk yourself out of going, or your clients, staff, or family will require your time and keep you from doing what you need to do to help yourself. Will you read business books, study, or prepare what you may need for the day to keep your business pushing forward? Arrive at the office before everyone else? Time-block your schedule so that you can complete a specific task at a specific time to stay on track for the day?

When you truly desire success, then you'll do everything in your power to make success a reality. You'll call prospects and generate leads, do social media videos to promote your business, send handwritten notes and mailout flyers to the community, study your field to become the expert, and complete all the important marketing to-dos to push tomorrow's sales forward. If you have a chance to read Brian Tracy's book, "Eat the Frog," it reinforces the idea of how important it is to complete all the dreaded duties of the day first for your business. **The morning should be time-blocked for generating, promoting, and enhancing tomorrow's business. Winning your first round today by owning your morning propels your business forward.**

In the business world, you deal with many different people and schedules throughout the day, so you must at least protect your morning schedule to prevent others from stealing it from you.

By owning your morning, you own the day. By owning your day, you own the weeks, months, and years...If you own the years, you own your life. And it all starts by controlling your morning. Set the pace for the day, week, and month to guarantee that you're supporting tomorrow's business first.

In addition to controlling your morning, you must control your marketing. **If you spend the first three hours of your morning marketing, prospecting, and generating more business, then you're planning for tomorrow's business and building your success.** Tomorrow's business will keep you in the business, so prepare for tomorrow's business by marketing today.

I had no idea where to start with marketing when I thought about starting a gym business, so my original approach was to spend little money on marketing and more money on resources for the gym. I told Dad about my vision for the gym, and his wise response to me was simply this, "Tim, you could have a cookout for 100 people but if the people don't know you're cooking, then nobody shows up." If no one knew my business existed, no one would show up.

The more you market, the more people will know your business exists, and the more clients you will have. Simple. People won't use your product if they don't know you are in the business.

Your job as a business owner or team leader is to make sure that the people know you are cooking for them. **Make sure everyone knows you're in the business, you have their best interests in mind, and that you'll work hard to deliver your product**. Advertise. Plan for tomorrow's business by spending your time today prospecting, marketing, and telling everyone you are cooking. If you own your morning and marketing, then you're already winning the first round of your day and winning for tomorrow's business.

Chapter 9 - Pray for the Best, Prepare for the Worst

"Everybody's got a plan until they get punched in the face."
(Mike Tyson)

"Life's not about how hard you hit, but how hard you can get
hit and keep moving forward." (Rocky Balboa)

Business does not go as planned. Just like a fight.

I can be a seasoned striker but when someone hits me with a
walled right hand, it takes me out of my game plan any day. It forces
me to fight relying more on instinct than strategy. Sometimes my
original strategy still works, but sometimes it doesn't.

In one of the fights I had taken short notice in a win-streak, I
was the dominant striker with a good wrestling and ground game and
my opponent was a bad striker, but expert wrestler. I was prepared
for a good fight but unprepared for the level of wrestling he brought
on the night of the fight. His wrestling against a good striker was
perfected and he disrupted my game plan. He took me so far out of
my game and so far into deep water that he drowned me, and proved
that I was under-prepared and over-confident.

Ripping an opponent away from his original game plan is
always the best way to win a fight. I have taken seasoned grapplers
and chosen to strike them specifically in a way that diminishes their
fighting ability because of the surprise distraction. It derails them
from their original game plan and they're left unprepared to adapt to
the worst-case scenario.

Nothing goes perfectly in business. Ever. **It doesn't matter
how fool-proof you think your game plan is, you always must
plan for things to go wrong.** Put contingencies in place to pick up
the slack when things do go wrong. Be ready. You can prepare all

you want to for a perfect execution of the plan, but if you do not also prepare for back-up plans, then you'll be left high and dry when the unexpected hits you in the face.

Ask for the opinion of others and evaluate the worst and best case scenarios. Even evaluate the most likely scenario. Run through each scenario and make sure that others on your team know back-up plans A, B, and C. **Your team and business must have a plan in place that can withstand the worst, the best, and the most likely.**

There are obviously aspects of any plan that can go wrong, and to expect perfection in a fallen world is naive. **Don't get caught with your hands in your pockets unprepared for the fight. This can be devastating to your business, income, and time.** You can remake money and memory but no one can make up for lost time, so plan well to protect your time.

In golf, if everyone was hell bent on making a hole-in-one every game then no one would ever play golf. Let's be real. A hole-in-one is so rare that no one would want to play if they couldn't achieve one every game. If you knock the golf ball into the sand trap or water, you keep trying to hit it back on track to the goal. The purpose of the game is to hit the golf ball as close to the hole with as few putts as possible, and adapt each time if the goal is not accomplished. Just like in business.

The hole is the victory, and everyone wants to get there as fast as possible. But if your business doesn't adapt to roadblocks along the way and is still swinging at putt twenty, then it'll always continue to swing. **It won't get anywhere since it isn't adapting to challenges or preparing for the worst-case scenario.**

Keep aiming at the goal no matter what comes your way.

Just like in golf, businesses carry large bags of tools and everyone (usually) has the same tools available, but this does not make all businesses equal on the playing ground. Tiger Woods plays with the same golf clubs as anyone else, but I'm sure you would agree that there is a large difference in the result of his dominating game over anyone else. **Own your tools and strategies and you will build skill. Work on improving your skill and you will become the expert.** Everyone has the same twenty-four hours available to them in a day, yet some people are successful and some are not. Everything depends on what each person is doing in those twenty-four hours.

There are plans and systems that won't work like you thought they would. But that doesn't mean that you must forfeit the game and give up on them altogether.

Sometimes there are alternate routes that must be taken. Let's say I'm traveling from where I live in Atlanta to my expansion real estate team's office in Johnson City, Tennessee. If there is a roadblock half-way there, then I do not stop, turn around, retreat, and say, "Well, I guess I'm not going to Tennessee today." I find another way around the roadblock and keep pushing through towards the goal. **There is always another way to meet the goal when the worst-case scenario arises**. Do not give up on yourself, your team or your business. Plan for best case, the worst case, and the most likely case scenario.

Train your instinct to calmly adapt when a situation goes sideways. Pray for the best but prepare for anything that may come along unexpectedly and upset your original game plan.

Chapter 10 - The Power of the Right Question

Every good fighter asks good questions. How do I need to prepare for my next fight? What technique do I need to master for the win? What are my strong points and weak points? What are my opponent's strong and weak points? How can I execute the best tactics to capitalize on his weaknesses? Questions like these bring reflection, focus, and growth to the fighter and help him prepare to take the win.

As soon as a fighter becomes cocky or overconfident, they stop asking these questions. **When they stop asking these questions, they stop reflecting, focusing, and growing. When they stop reflecting, focusing, and growing, they become weak.** And no athlete can afford any weak spells. When an athlete hits a weak spell their mindset changes. Instead of keeping a mindset that fosters growth, they develop a negative mindset that either justifies their poor level of ability, becomes over confident and prideful of their ability, or they quit altogether. **Any level of this weak spell damages their long-term game and success. Pride, discouragement, and loss are the biggest contributors to deaf ears toward wise counsel.** If an athlete grows prideful or finds themselves too discouraged, or if they quit altogether, they'll get their ass kicked and still fail to listen and learn.

When anyone stops seeking growth, they damage their future success.

The message is simple. **Ask questions to generate growth and refuse to become cocky or underconfident.** Either extreme is dangerous. Quitting is out of the question. Focus on your goals no matter the circumstances and ask hard questions. **Get into the habit now of asking questions to bring focus to your business and further its growth.** Ask yourself, what do I need to do to bring my business to the next level? What can I change now to improve my future business? What do I need to improve for my clients and customers? Questions keep your business moving. The moment you stop asking them is the moment you decide that you want your business to fail.

Don't ask any question with the intention of hearing the answer you want to hear, ask questions with the intentions of hearing truth, and the truth will force you to grow.

If you are surrounded by people who never offer constructive criticism to your systems, ideas, and game plans, then you're not surrounded by game changers. The "yes sir, yes ma'am" people who never question you will always give you the answers you want to hear. Although these team members are helpful to have on the team, they are unhelpful when it comes to asking questions to further growth. You're surrounded by people who don't want to hurt you, so you're not getting the full truth from them when you ask questions.

You need to uncover the full truth to hard questions in order to scale your business and reach its fullest potential.

Ask your closest friends the hard, reflective questions about your business. Listen to their advice and apply it appropriately (even if they are not experts in the field, their opinion still matters). An outside opinion can be priceless for the growth of your business, so seek it and be willing to learn from it. Those on the outside are seeing things from a perspective you will never be able to.

If you stop asking questions to generate future growth, then prepare for your weak spell since it will come. Remember that in this question-asking-growth-process you will be uncomfortable and it won't be easy at first. Get used to it. **Growth pains are never fun but they are bring breakthroughs, focus, and wins.** If you want to be successful then ask the hard questions to generate growth in your business, even when you do not like the answers given.

Chapter 11 - Saying Yes Means Saying No

When fighters say "yes" to a fight, they automatically say "yes" to more training and "no" to other commitments. When fighters say "no" to a fight, they automatically say "yes" to other obligations.

There are some people who cannot say "no" to anyone or any obligation, so they fill their schedule with over-commitments and tedious activities that they really don't want to do, but they couldn't say no to. Others say "yes" now but turn around and say "no" after they realize they were too quick to say "yes." Others just say "no" to everything. Which of these people are you? You may not want to admit it, but you fit into one of these categories.

The "yes" or "no" decision is sometimes a difficult one, but it always must be made and automatically *is* made every time anyone says "no" or "yes." Understand that if you say "no" to an evening out on the town, then you say "yes" to an evening at home. If you say "no" to one job, you say "yes" to another job. If you say "yes" to an obligation at a specific time, then you say "no" to another obligation at that time since you can't do two things at once. Although people don't typically think too philosophically about what their answer means, it is important to understand that these simple words can turn the course of your productivity 180 degrees and bring your business guaranteed success.

This decision guarantees that you'll be led down a black and white path of success or failure. When you say "yes" to certain people and non-income producing tasks, you're automatically saying "no" to other people and tasks who could have required your attention in an income-producing activity. **When you say "yes" to a non-income producing activity, you are automatically saying**

"no" to an income producing activity that could be forwarding the business to success.

This ideology challenges us to be cautious in decision making as we build a scalable and sell-able business. **Focusing on systems, procedures, training, and education to build a scalable and sell-able business says "NO" to inefficient systems, poor training, and a faulty foundation for your business.** Saying "YES" to furthering education and self-growth says "YES" to income producing activities.

No one can take away your ambition to grow and succeed. When you say "YES" to activities that exercise your ambition, will-power muscle, and discipline, then you are automatically saying "NO" to time vacuums that decrease the productivity of your business. You must make the decision for yourself every day, over and over again determining what you will say "yes" and "no" to in your business. No one can make these decisions for you. Teach your team members to make the right decision in their "yes" and "no" battles as well by leading from example. Assess what activities will be income producing and beneficial for your business. Cut out the activities that are non-income producing and spend more time on the activities that will increase your productivity levels.

Here is a challenge that you can easily implement in your business and pass along to your team members. Create a chart that includes fifteen minute time increments for two days from nine o'clock in the morning to five o'clock in the evening. Next to the fifteen minute time blocks, create empty spaces for a one word answer. Challenge your team members to set a timer for every fifteen minutes from nine to five for two days, to alarm them to take a break from what they are doing and assess the last fifteen minutes of their work. Were they working on income producing activities? Prospecting and generating business? Meeting with clients, making calls, negotiating business for tomorrow's success? Marketing, networking, or creating advertisements on social media? Or were they doing less income producing activities and filing paperwork, making copies, brainstorming, finishing a project, or completing any administration work or training? Were they browsing on social media, chatting with work buddies, or taking too many bathroom breaks to watch funny videos or play games? Figure out what the various income producing activities are in your business and rank the various activities from "great," "good," or "bad" for the business. Even if everyone holds themselves highly accountable to a strict schedule, the first day of the challenge will be a rude awakening to how much "bad" or "good" is happening and how little "great" is happening in the business, or how much discipline has been lacking in their daily schedule.

This challenge will help you and your team say "YES" to income producing activities and forward the success of the business to create a scalable and sell-able business. **Say "no" to negativity and laziness. Say "no" to everything detrimental to your business. When you say "no" to these activities, you train yourself to say "YES" to more discipline and more income producing activities.**

Chapter 12 - Do Not Touch the Wood Twice

Do you remember a time in your life when you learned a simple lesson that changed your life? Maybe a mentor, preacher or teacher instilled in you a valuable lesson that you still use today. It could have been a simple lesson, but you still needed someone else to teach it to you. You may never have been enlightened to remember the lesson unless they critiqued your system or gave you a consequence that helped you remember the lesson.

I remember one day growing up I helped my dad and uncle unload wood from a truck so that they could split it for firewood. I threw the wood pieces out of their truck, piled them on the ground, then carried them over to my dad and uncle and re-stacked for them to cut. A few minutes passed as my dad watched me work, then after thinking a moment he said, "Tim, you're touching every piece of wood twice before you stack it which requires more of your time and energy, and it is not the most efficient way to work." A simple point that any bystander may have observed, but in doing the action, I couldn't see that it was not the most efficient way. Instead of stacking the wood by the truck, then moving the piles to re-stack, I needed to remove the first step and make the process much simpler.

Even in the small task of stacking wood and splitting it, there needed to be a more efficient system to save my time and energy. Cutting out a small step in the process allowed more productive activity in the long run, but I needed someone else to show me that was needed.

My dad not only taught me a lesson in productivity that day, but also a lesson in taking criticism. If you can't take criticism then you'll never grow. **Fighters need to be trainable before they taste success.** Although I tend to be very hardheaded and I like doing things my own way, I had to be taught that **being a good worker**

comes before becoming a great leader, and being a good worker includes taking criticism.

We complete tasks either out of habit or according to our own interpretation of the best way to get something done before someone teaches us how to do it better. We can do something the same way for twenty years and never consider a better way of doing it until someone proves to us that their way is better. We can complete small tasks and not consider a procedure or system that would save us a small ounce of time and energy in the long run.

When authorities offer a more efficient way of doing things, the ability to listen well and implement their constructive criticism to improve our productivity is key to our success. This teaches us to become good, efficient workers and stronger fighters before we become great leaders. If you are a leader and you cannot take any constructive criticism from others, prepare to fail in your business and leadership. You must listen to the bystanders who may offer a better, more efficient way for you to handle your business. You cannot be the best in your field if you cannot listen to others and grow in areas that you may be lacking.

This story's second application to business is simple. **Make sure people do things right the first time so that tasks don't have to be corrected by someone else, or even done completely over again.** Touching the wood twice takes more time and energy. Systems and procedures are in place for everything to be done right the first time, or as close to it as possible. **Teach your team to work most efficiently in their assigned tasks and systems, and to listen well when others may offer a better system.**

Doing the same task twice is the absolute worst return on your time, and your time is the number one commodity that can never be repaid. When your team learns to work more efficiently the first time, you'll be amazed at how much more productivity your business will soon accomplish.

Chapter 13 - You Cannot Overstretch What You Cannot Afford

Your pocketbook may not allow you to live at the limit of luxury you desire. But your cost of living may increase in relation to your pay raises at work. Or you may choose to live below your limit of luxury to save more money for the future. Whether your ideal shopping spree is at a grocery store, the Mall, a bookstore, an athletic store, or the like, you justify spending money on certain things but avoid spending money on other items... No matter what your spending or saving habits are, we all have them and they dictate how we live.

If you look at someone's checkbook, friends, schedule, and books they read, you can estimate where they will be in five years. This shows you what is important enough to them for them to spend their money and time on every day.

The financial habits we have now dictate whether or not we will be more successful or barely scraping by in a few years down the road.

When my wife and I first opened the gym, Moab Fighting Concepts, I barely had enough money and only minimal equipment available for the new business. We had to start the business small, equivalent to the resources at our disposal. It would have been foolish at the time to buy a building too big for our pocketbook with equipment too expensive for what we needed. If we had gone that route, then we would not have had the available resources to grow into a bigger business since we would've been wallowing in debt for ages.

So we started small with what we could afford. Basic finance. Starting small allowed us to slowly grow into a bigger business which would never have been possible if we had tried to start a big business on a low budget. The gym has moved three different times to better suit its needs. **Spending only the money we needed allowed us to save the money we needed for the expansion and growth of the business with much less risk.** Although we could have tried to start a big business on a low budget, the risk and debt to income ratio would have been too high for us to see any positive return on the investment for a long time. Not to mention the foolishness of the decision. **Overstretching what a business cannot afford misuses its time, finances, and resources, and highly increases its risk of detrimental failure.**

My real estate business has grown from a one-person office, to a double office, to an office suite, to an office building with an expansion team. We started small but grew and moved into bigger offices as our business grew. Our financial bookkeeping, training, and schedules all reflected our vision for growth. We invested our time and money into what we decided was important without overstretching what we couldn't afford.

You may have been saving for future growth for a while now, but you may not be sure when to gauge if your business has hit a next level of growth. **Businesses must think and act wisely when it comes to their financial planning. It is wise to keep a minimum of six months of finances in reserve for anything that might happen.** A business is wisely living inside of feasible financial limits when it keeps a financial cushion for emergencies. If a business has calculated the expense for its expansion and achieved in its savings account the expansion cost multiplied by six (since they will need six months of finances in reserve), it may be an appropriate time to start planning and implementing expansion. Once a business gains any amount of debt, it becomes easier for that business to lessen the discipline of maintaining strict finances. What a vicious cycle this becomes for the business! It becomes nearly impossible for the business to crawl out of a pit of debt. Your business should not overspend or overstretch what it does not have or else it will crumble beneath debt.

Chapter 14 - Get Used to Being Uncomfortable

When you are challenged to step outside a comfort zone in any regard, you experience a sense of growth and accomplishment when you complete the challenge. The feelings of doubt and discomfort that initially overwhelmed you disappear in the shadow of the success that appears when you overcome the challenge.

It was comfortable for me to rely on the same training partners when I prepared for various fights. However, when I relied on the same training partners for different fights, the partners not only figured out which techniques I favored, but I also figured out which techniques they favored. My training partners failed to challenge me in new techniques and varied levels of fighting. I discovered the best way to beat my training partners so my training just became normal practice with no new challenge or obstacle.

I felt well prepared against a great opponent in Atlanta since I had trained and defeated my training partners time and again. I was comfortable with the techniques and well-practiced in what I thought I needed. But when I faced my opponent in the ring, I realized that I lacked a training partner with the level of experience I needed to prepare me well for this fight. I had not leveled up in my training. My fighting was only as good as my training had been, and I had not stepped out of my comfort zone to receive the level of training I needed to meet the higher standard for this fight. And that was my fault.

In business, you must step out of your comfort zone in order to challenge your team and increase to the next level. The business will only be as good as its systems, procedures, and staff, so **you must continually level them up to make sure that the business is achieving its highest level of success through the challenge.**

I remember the first time my real estate team had twenty pending contracts at once. Every system we had originally created was broken to hell. Nothing worked the way it was supposed to. The systems and procedures were not structured well enough to support any growth in business. When we scaled up the systems and procedures in the team to handle growth, we scaled up our business. The amount of business we had before growth was comfortable, but what is comfortable at twenty transactions will be uncomfortable at fifty transactions.

When you downsize your business it is easy, but when you expand it will be uncomfortable. If you want growth, you need to be challenged. Get uncomfortable to scale your systems and procedures, and handle well the growth that your business needs to succeed. This is not up to anyone else besides you. You are responsible for leveling up and strengthening your will-power to step outside of your comfort zone.

No one has ever achieved greatness or high levels of success without first being uncomfortable. Think of a staircase with 1,000 steps. Climbing up the stairs is a challenge, but when it levels out to a landing area when the systems and procedures are put in place, you will see the rewarding success brought by the challenge. **When you have a scalable business, you will have sell-able results.** Don't get comfortable in your current business. When you complete the 1,000-step staircase, look for a 10,000-step staircase to climb. **Always challenge the way you think and the systems you implement so that your business can be challenged to the next level of growth.** Don't get cozy and comfortable, get *ahead*. Grow. Succeed. And look for more ways to challenge the business when it does succeed.

Shake the tree to cause the fruit to fall and then find another tree. This process will be uncomfortable! But you must scale the business and hire more people, seek to make the business greater, and the team more uncomfortable. Get used to being uncomfortable and challenging your team to reach new breakthroughs, since this will catapult the business to reach new horizons never dreamed of before.

Your team's vision of growth will echo your vision of growth, so your vision must be built on this challenge if you want your team's vision to be challenged for growth.

Level up, start training with a more challenging training partner, and accept the challenges that can grow your business to the next level. You will be rewarded with accomplishments and successes – and even if you fail, you will learn. This is the key to building a scalable business with sell-able results that succeeds at high levels.

Chapter 15 - Your Strongest Attribute As An Entrepreneur Is...

It is no uncommon fact that the mind is a powerful being and that we are only as strong as our minds allow us to be. Have you heard the stories of hikers climbing Mt. Everest in flip-flops with no protective gear? Although this is impossible according to all science and previous attempts, some hikers succeeded solely because of their mindset and determination. People who have never ran a mile commit to running ultramarathons and set records in their success. They may run until their body shuts down, but will keep running until their goal is met because their mindset is unbeatable. There are so many incredible stories of people successfully completing impossible activities because of their determination and strong mindset.

In the fighting ring, the fighter with the highest level of determination and strongest mindset always wins.

In the same way, the boldest attribute anyone could ever hold as an entrepreneur is a strong mindset. **The mind and its determination are often greatly under estimated in business**. However, if you learn to take advantage of a good, strong mindset and leverage its determination toward your business, while teaching others to keep a strong, healthy mindset, then your business will be unstoppable.

The secret to succeeding in any business does not depend on a wealth of resources or the bulge of a big muscle in the face of competition, the secret to success is dependent on a strong team mindset and strengthening that mindset no matter the circumstances. Your team could be the smallest team in the business with the smallest amount of exposure and lowest resource or marketing budget, but it could have a determined mindset and because of that mindset, your team will crush every other team ten times out of ten.

If you surround yourself with people who believe the glass to be half empty then you will adapt to their negative mindset. The same is true if you surround yourself with people who believe the glass to be half full. So, you must ensure that your mindset is as strong or stronger than the mindsets of those with whom you surround yourself.

If you are stranded in the ocean and are given a flotation device you will stay afloat, but if you are stranded and given an anchor, you will sink. Do not surround yourself with negativity, discontentment, or a pessimistic mindset or you will sink faster than a heavy weight. **You must spend your time and energy focusing on building a positive mindset and surrounding yourself with floaters, not anchors.** Positive mindsets will lift your spirits and bring hope in all areas of life, not just in regards to your business. Positivity will build a strong mindset and negativity will destroy one.

Many of us tell ourselves lies every day that hold us back from new opportunities and hinder our success. For instance, we've surely all told ourselves: *You're not good enough. You'll never make it in this business. Everyone else is better at this than you are.* **What lies are you telling yourself every day that are keeping you pinned under the thumb of mediocrity, negativity, and hindering your success?**

Instead of saying that you're not good enough, remind yourself that you bring a new perspective to the business that no one else can bring. Rephrase any negativity into positivity. You *will* make it in the business since no one else has control over your ambition or work ethic except for you. With your hard work and discipline, you *will* be the best that you can be in this business. Focus your energy on improving your strengths instead of beating yourself up over your weaknesses. Take a minute to rephrase the lies you hear into truths you can believe.

I remember when I quit high school as a sophomore to start working as a fulltime film salvage, people told me I would never succeed in life. They planted doubts in my mind about the direction my life would follow, and were quick to tell me lies that I would never amount to anything. There were times I believed their lies. But the route that I took taught me the work ethic, time management, and respect for authorities that I needed to learn, I needed to take that route in order to grow and succeed. **Sometimes, the less traveled road can be a hidden route to success and can be unique to your needs, even if the circumstance appears negative.** If you focus on your strengths and ignore other people's expectations and opinions, you may find yourself on a less traveled road to success.

The mind is so powerful that it can make champions out of the impossible, and at the same time it can tragically convince others that there is no purpose and no hope left in life. With the right mindset, there is nothing too great that cannot be conquered in this life. No trial too great, no tragedy too catastrophic, no situation too dire that could ever make you so hopeless that you decide to quit your ambitions entirely or even worse, end your life. **It is not the weight of a situation that brings hopelessness, it is a poisonous mindset.**

Some of the greatest people in this world have been through hell and back, yet their mindset remains one of peace, wisdom, and utmost determination to influence others to succeed and do good in this world. Some of the most successful people I know have experienced the greatest tragedies. Some of the most religious people I know have experienced horrid events, yet their mindset is one of continued trust and peace in the Lord. These people are testaments to the mind's power and determination. My intention here is not to diminish the gravity of tragedy so do not misunderstand. I have personally experienced many a tragedy in my own life and fully understand its capabilities, and my condolences are sent to you if the timing of these words is forlorn. My point is that when we maintain a strong mindset, even when tragedies hit, they will not overcome us. **If we maintain a strong mindset we can become champions of the impossible and grow stronger emotionally, physically, spiritually, and cognitively, in our businesses, and in all other areas of life.** We will be strong. We will not quit. We will determine never to forfeit ourselves to a weak mindset.

We must want a strong mindset in order to own a strong mindset. If you do not want it badly enough then it will be impossible for you to build a strong mindset. Your mindset will also be contagious among your team members, so if you want a more positive team, then start setting the example yourself. **Want it. Own it. Grow it.** And as you grow, your determination and positivity will surprise you.

If you would like to read an inspiring book about building a strong mindset with no excuses, I recommend reading *Can't Hurt Me* by David Goggins and applying it every day to your life and business.

Chapter 16 - Mind What Matters

I didn't feel like I needed more training for the fight, but my coach disagreed. My coach, Casey Oxendine, was preparing me for a fight that would take place in the high elevation of mountainous Colorado. Since the air is thinner and the environmental conditions restrict oxygen, if someone is not used to working out or fighting at a higher elevation, then he has an automatic disadvantage to his opponent who may already be adapted to the area.

Coach kept saying that the higher altitude would have a greater effect on me than I was anticipating . . . but I remained skeptical. He'd already trained me well in various conditions, so I felt more than well-prepared.

As soon as we arrived in Colorado, I could already tell the difference in my breathing. I only had two days to shed twenty pounds before the fight (something I definitely don't miss from the fighting world) so I headed to the gym for a good workout. When I started my cardio, I immediately felt fatigued. It was horrible. It felt like someone had placed a 500-pound vest on my chest. I'd trained so hard for the fight and yet in this moment I felt so unprepared and out of breath. This was going to be one of the top fights in my career and I couldn't even catch my breath riding a bike in the gym!

My attempt to focus on endurance and conditioning wasn't going to help me at this altitude. Coach saw my fatigue and disappointment and stopped me. Rather than chanting *I told ya' so,* he said, "I want you to focus on three things in the fight. Hit hard, be first, and give it all you got. The altitude won't matter if you can shorten the fight."

When it was time to fight, I remembered his words and focused on that first minute.

In twenty seconds, the fight was over. And boy, was I thankful that I didn't have to fight for another twenty minutes at 6,000 ft. above sea level.

I knocked out the opponent because I listened to my coach and focused on a high level of aggression and concentration within the first minute. Before the fight I was so focused on conditioning and endurance that I would've lost the fight if my coach hadn't wisely redirected my focus to the importance of that first minute. He taught me to focus on what mattered for this fight, and disregard everything else.

A lot of us have heard the phrase "mind over matter." But rather than just believing in "mind over matter," it's important to first "mind *what* matters" so that your focus and initiative will be concentrated on what is needed for the win without distraction.

At the time of the fight, I couldn't physically prepare any more than I already had, no matter how much "mind over matter" capability I could've kicked into gear. Due to my lack of preparation, it was just too late to meet Colorado-breathing standards, so the only option was for my coach to focus my strategy. Ultimately if I hadn't focused on strategy I would have misapplied my focus and lost the fight. When I applied my focus in the right area for the right fight, the win came easy; but the only way for me to attain the win was to "mind what mattered."

If you fail to focus your attention on what is important for your life and business, then you may find yourself in a situation that no matter how much "mind *over* matter" you employ, you will still lose the fight. You can almost always avoid losses with a "mind **what** matters" mindset. "Minding **what** matters" sometimes requires a measure of "mind *over* matter," but most of all it requires the discipline to strengthen your mindset and ignore what does not matter so you can focus on what does, with a high level of concentration and initiative.

When I was a kid, I remember taking a magnifying glass to start a fire by directing the sunlight to one specific point in the grass. I may have burned one too many patches in my backyard, but I learned to direct the sun's power into energy. What you choose to magnify in your business will become hot and fiery, powerful and great because of the intense focus you dedicate to make it great. **When you direct your attention and maximize your energy toward what matters to the vision and mission statement of the business you are in, you can magnify momentum and attain the win.** You mind what matters when you direct your power and momentum where they need to be, and away from non-income producing activities and negativity.

Since what you choose to focus on will become magnified in your life, focusing on what is positive and upbuilding will help you mind what matters to disregard the negativity that does not edify your business.

Comparing two different roads will not get you to your own destination any faster, so when you *mind* **your own path to success and** *stop minding* **your competitor's path to his success,** you'll quicken your pace in your own journey to success. Your road to success may include the stepping stones of obtaining more education, finally accepting a career change, hiring more staff for your team, or recognizing your weaknesses with more transparency. All of these stepping stones will look differently than your competitors' stepping stones.

Remember that **anyone can put their mind to something great, unthinkable even, and achieve it if they mind what matters and disregard what does not matter.**

If we give our time, energy, and attention to the wrong things, we will end up losing the fight. If you're exhausting yourself trying to succeed and you're not getting anywhere, then it may be time to shift your magnifying glass and assess what activities need to be winning your focus.

- What actions are you doing that are not important for your business? Are you exerting your power and focus on the wrong activities?
- Are you listening to lies that hinder your success? Are you letting negativity win your mindset?
- Are you focusing on your own path to success or someone else's? What or who may be hindering you from taking the first step in your route to success?

Magnifying your momentum to the income-producing activities and values that matter to the business allow you to hone in on your strategy and focus on the win. Rephrase the lies you may be telling yourself about your future into positive truths that re-shape your future of success. When you focus on believing positive truths about your business, they will be magnified in your actions and ultimately lead to your success. Refusing to lose and pushing yourself one step farther than you think you can down the pathway to your success helps you mind what matters and not mind what doesn't matter.

Chapter 17 - Position Over Submission

Within the world of Brazilian Jiu Jitsu, the focus of any fighter should remain on controlling his position in a fight. If the fighter loses control of his position, then his opponent will submit him ("submitting" is a term used to signify a fighter giving up to his opponent) and conquer him in the fight. If the fighter dives in for the submission of his opponent too soon in the fight, then he risks losing control. Forfeiting the upper hand and control of his position could cost him the victory. However, if he maintains control of his position, then submission of his opponent can seamlessly occur.

We must always work to control our position in the field of business we're in. **Our position = our systems and procedures that bring success. Controlling our position is more important than trying to be the top of the market.**

Focus on your systems and procedures, and you will see the upward course of growth. Do not start new systems and procedures before you master your old ones, or you may forfeit the business's position and upper hand.

If your team starts ten new systems, they can give 10% to all of them. If they start only one system, they can give 100% of their energy, time, and resources to fully implement that one system successfully before they create additional procedures. If the new system or procedure is a complete flop, then your team can immediately fall back to what was working before the implementation of that specific system. But, if your team loses its focus and dives in for the top of the market too early by launching many new systems at one time, then your whole business will fall to pieces. It will lose control and won't be able to clean up that big of a mess while also scrambling for the win—its focus will be diverted in fixing ten failed systems versus fixing one failed system. **Solve**

simple problems to maintain your control. When you forfeit your control, you forfeit the win.

Remember, your business focuses on will become magnified. If your team focuses on implementing one new system at a time, that system will be so thoroughly understood and implemented by the team that it will take no time for everyone to adjust to the change.

Know what you know and learn what you do not know one step at a time. Do not try learning every new thing at once. Succeed at the tried and true systems and then add one new system at a time. Don't overwhelm your staff by trying to teach the business twenty new things at once or they will forget, get sloppy, rush haphazardly in confusion, and lose the overall vision and focus of the business. **Keep your team focused on one new lesson, one new system or procedure, or one new vision at a time. Keep focused on the control of your business.**

Keep focused on the current procedures and systems until they are mastered before adding more. Then add one new procedure at a time, building onto the success of the team and controlling its position so that you don't leave any man behind.

Do not try to win the game of chess without strategizing every move and keeping your focus stabilized one move at a time. When you fight with a position-over-submission mindset, you'll stabilize your business and attain the win.

Chapter 18 - Are You a champ?

Professional fighters and other athletes do not wake up every morning and tell themselves that they could never be a champion or never succeed in their career. They wake up every morning and tell themselves that they are the champion of champions. They believe that truth, and it helps them push harder for the win. When they follow up with the actions and habits to support this belief, the world believes them to be the champion of champions that they claim to be.

Whether we like it or not, we are what we believe. **Our beliefs form the habits and behaviors that we exhibit, which dictate the words we say and ultimately the person that others perceive us to be.** If you believe that it is important to be kind to others, you may give a compliment or show kindness to a co-worker, and they will perceive you to be a kind person. When we act upon what we believe to be true, others' perceptions of us develop accordingly.

We all hold a specific belief system that dictates the actions we exhibit and the person we become. Do you believe that you are worth something and will succeed as a champion? You may claim to believe this, but you may not have the actions or habits in place reflecting the ideology to make this happen. When you reflect this belief in your speech and actions, you set an example for others in your business, and ultimately change the entire mindset and orientation of the business.

When you believe you are a champion, you will form habits and behaviors that forward your goals and lead to your success.

This happens with anything you do. **If you believe something to be true, you expect it to happen and plan appropriately to make it happen.** This is also called a self-fulfilling prophecy. If you believe you'll fail an exam, you'll most likely fail. If you believe you'll excel on an exam, you'll most likely excel if you've also appropriately studied out of the belief that you will excel.

We are all stronger and capable of so much more than we think we can handle. **If we fill our minds with pessimistic lies that will never move us forward, then we will always be pulled backwards, away from our goals and success.** If we fill our minds with positive truths to propel us forward, then we will always be one step closer to achieving our goals, successes, and the ultimate win.

Coach taught me as a young fighter that we can't fill our minds with a bad diet of negativity and expect healthy, positive results. If I was pessimistic about a fight, I was more likely to lose. If I kept a positive outlook, I was more likely to win. I needed to keep my end-goal in sight in every fight in order to keep a positive outlook. If I lost sight of my end goal, I would not fight as hard in the ring. But if I kept my end goal as the fuel to my fighting fire, I was motivated to make each move count.

Believe that you will win, train to win, and you'll be more apt to win. Apply the same mindset to your business and you'll change your future.

We choose every day whether or not we'll fuel the fire of momentum to reach our goals, or douse that fire out. The lies and negativity that we may choose to believe douse that fire out, hindering us from attaining our goals, successes, and ultimate win.

We are only as good as what we allow ourselves to be. If we believe that we are great and will do great things, our actions will reflect that belief.

If your business believes that customers and clients always come first, that they truly do matter, then this belief will drive the business's goals and will be reflected with the right follow-through actions.

Your personal life and business will naturally reflect the values and ideologies that you believe. When businesses abide by their values and morals, every day is a step in the right direction. When they believe that their business has a great purpose, they'll act confidently in relation to that great purpose. If you don't know the values of the business, then you're less likely to act with purpose toward its goals, or be motivated fueling your fire to succeed. It is so important to communicate the business's beliefs clearly to all team members to make sure everyone is fighting toward the same goal. When everyone is on board with the business's beliefs, then everyone will be on board with the goals and actions to achieve its success.

You can teach people a lot of lessons, but you cannot teach someone a change in beliefs. They must come to those realizations on their own. Even though you cannot make them understand beliefs, you can *show* others your beliefs by living them out.

When leadership sets the right example, the team will learn how the right beliefs can propel the business to success. You are what you believe and your team will become what they believe. When you feed your mindset the right diet, the right results will follow.

Are you a champion? Do you believe your team is full of champions? **Believe it, enact the habits and behaviors to show it, then everyone will naturally know it.** This will help lead the business to a culture of success.

Chapter 19 - Circle Around, Do Not Retreat

Soldiers, Navy Seals, Marines, and other Military personnel have always amazed me at their bravery and courage to move forward toward the enemy or danger no matter what. They do not retreat unless they are told. They are always ready to sacrifice their lives for others. They are an entirely different breed of humans than most of us can relate to. We are apt to forget what these men risk everyday in their service and honor to their country protecting others' lives, rights, values, and freedoms. They teach us important lessons in discipline and bravery, and they'll always be the experts in exhibiting these values and more.

I'd like to focus on an important aspect of their ideology that pushes them forward and never backward. They never retreat unless the circumstances absolutely demand it, and even then they have the systems and procedures implemented so that a man is never left behind. They completely function as one organism.

Retreating leaves men vulnerable for an attack. In this position, men are nothing more than sitting ducks since the opponent knows exactly where the men are headed and can expose and capitalize on their vulnerability.

This lesson is also taught to fighters and boxers. One of the first lessons I learned in combat from my two boxing coaches – the late Cobb Riddle and the late Marvin Fritts - was to circle around my opponent allowing me to avoid any of their weapons while never backing myself into a corner. Circling around the opponent gave me a superior angle to attack. This technique is a much better alternative than backing into a corner since retreating is a defensive move, never an offensive move.

The business application is simple. **Once you have a goal in sight, never back away from that goal.** This doesn't mean running into an obstacle unprepared, but rather never retreating when an obstacle does present itself. Assess the situation and determine the best route around (or through) the obstacle. Circle around the obstacle or goal. **Take the superior position, do not retreat or give up. Fight until you hit that goal and then keep fighting toward the next goal; fight until you win.**

As the saying goes, there is more than one way to skin a cat, so do not give up completely if you meet an obstacle on your way to achieve your team's the goal. **Backing up, retreating, and completely giving up decreases morale and motivation.** Whereas circling around the goal allows you to keep an open mind about the path to reach the goal with a militant perspective about moving forward no matter what obstacle comes in the way.

If someone gets hit in a fight, it is okay that they've been hit. They don't forfeit the fight but they keep moving forward focused on their end goal. In the same way, when you are considering hiring new employees, if you make a bad hire and it hinders you from hitting your goal right away, do not back away from the goal. Just solve the problem by hiring someone else. If your team is experimenting with a new lead source and it is not working well for your team, then you shouldn't throw away the ultimate goal of generating leads.

If you face tribulation or turbulence along the way of reaching your goal, keep pushing through. If you're on an airplane and experience turbulence along the way, it would be foolish to jump out of the plane rather than persevere through the flight until you reach your destination.

So create new systems, new leads, new hires, new ways to reach your goal. Always keep moving forward.

Train your mind to circle around the goal instead of retreat. **This will train defeat out of the culture of your business and help you persevere until you make it to the end of the fight. Do not give up.**

Chapter 20 - Seemingly Unattainable Goals

Society teaches that goals must be realistic, achievable, and attainable, and some of you will hate this chapter because it will contradict this ideology. Making goals realistic, achievable, and attainable teaches us to settle for less than we may be capable of. **Why make a goal if you already see yourself achieving it? A goal needs to be so big that it requires many smaller steps to reach it.**

If you've become comfortable settling for laziness instead of discipline, then you will hate this chapter. If you think you're at the top of your game and cannot set any higher goals in your business, than you are wrong. **Your business may be on the verge of failing miserably due to a lack of appropriate goal-setting.** There is always more to learn and there are always more goals to set for your team.

Before I retired from fighting, I always wanted to make it to the international stage. The big payday. The glorious fight. I knew that this was a very lofty goal for me, however, because I was trying to work fulltime while fighting professionally. Reaching that high of a goal was nearly unattainable for me. But that did not keep my coach from training me to attain that farfetched goal—sometimes even against my will.

One long training day led to another long training day, then another, and another. My coach pushed me past my physical limits so much so that I thought I was going to die from exhaustion. Coach kept challenging me to stay consistent and work hard even when all I wanted to do was quit. He kept pushing me to stay consistent and work hard physically, mentally, and emotionally. It taught me how much potential our bodies have beyond the limits we set for ourselves. Coach helped me transition from a local pro-fighter to a national pro-fighter and although I did have an opportunity to fight internationally, it never panned out. But I wasn't disappointed, since the original unattainable goal had pushed me to achieve so many other great things that I never thought would be possible when I first started. The high unattainable goal didn't seem too farfetched after I went from the local level to the national level. And it especially didn't seem so unattainable when the opportunity finally presented itself to fight internationally.

I had hoped, dreamed, trained, and fought for this seemingly *UN*attainable goal. **When your goal is seemingly *UN*attainable - or at least *UN*attainable at the time when it was set - then you will be challenged to push yourself toward the next level.** When you make shitty goals you lock away the potential that can get you to the next breakthrough. By setting seemingly unattainable goals that exceed your expectations, you give yourself the constant motivation to tap into a well of potential that you didn't even know you had. **When you believe that you have more to give, then you *will* have more to give.** Once you stop limiting yourself with an "I can't do it" attitude, you'll already be five steps closer than you are right now to achieving the goal that you set.

Do you want to know how you can push your business to the next level? Start setting big ass goals that will specifically improve your business and foster its growth. Not vague goals, but specific goals. Goals that will hold you accountable to train harder. Work smarter. And re-work your systems to the best efficiency.

When you set your goals high you set your standards high, and you set your actions higher. Do your business a favor and give it more credit by setting seemingly unattainable goals for its success.

Let's say you make $50,000 dollars one year and decide to set what seems like the unattainable goal of earning $1 million dollars the next year. You work your ass off to boost all systems, scrub all leads, encourage and train all employees at a higher level of service, increase your profit twenty times by increasing the quality of your product, increase self-education and coaching, set actions to hit your big goal one step at a time, and so forth. At the end of that year, you look at the books and see that you've fallen short of making one million dollars—but you've made $800,000. Which is sixteen times better than the previous year when you only made $50,000. **At the time when you made the goal of earning $1 million it seemed highly unattainable, but it doesn't seem too farfetched when you make $800,000. In fact, now you could create an even higher goal and set your expectations even higher to push yourself even higher to the next breakthrough.**

It is better to fall a little short of making $1 million dollars than to make only $50,000. **If you set a goal that is nearly unattainable, and you set specific and trackable actions to obtain that goal, it is better to fall short of that big ass goal than to limit your potential by keeping your standards low.**

When we get comfortable we get lazy. When we "try our best" and give up, we forfeit the fight altogether because we were too lazy to push to the next level.

When you think you have made it to the top and you think you have no more goals to set, do not get cozy or you'll let the rookie pass you by. Always keep pushing yourself and your business to the next big ass goal. Aim for that unattainable goal and constantly re-assess your systems to sustain more growth.

You cannot attain true success until you fight every day to push past your limits with hard work and consistency. Exercise discipline. Hold each other accountable. And you will make possible what seems impossible for your life and business.

Chapter 21 - Measure Twice, Cut Once

My dad is a man of many talents and served as a master carpenter for furniture factories at one point in his life. He installed furniture equipment and supervised the workers to ensure processes were running properly and the products were created flawlessly. Unfortunately my father experienced a heart attack that limited his ability to continue working in this same position, so after his recovery, he began making wooden knick-knacks and small pieces of furniture at home instead. He offered me some money if I helped him, so I worked with him in carpentry for a time, hungry to make an extra penny.

His motto while we worked together was: "measure twice and cut once." I'm sure you can guess where this is going, but bear with me. If you only measure once and cut once, you may cut incorrectly. If you make a mistake in this step and make a wrong cut, then you not only ruin the cost of the wood but you also lose the profit from what the wood could have been made into. The overall product is ruined and the cost, work, and time is wasted. Measure twice and cut once.

We talked last chapter about setting seemingly *UN*attainable goals and why this is so important for challenging your business to the next level. There always needs to be a clear goal for your business, and everyone on the team needs to know what the goal is and why it is so important. There must be clear action steps to reach that goal, and everyone must know why, how, when, and who will be working toward achieving the goal to fully understand how the goal will come to fruition. Measure twice, cut once. Measure the steps that will work toward the potential achievement of the business's big ass goal. Then implement those action steps as flawlessly as possible. **If your business haphazardly aims to get**

somewhere with no motivation behind its action steps, no "WHY" behind the cut, then its measurements will be off and much time, work, and resources will be wasted in a failure. If the employees do not understand each step or why each step must be taken, there will be disunity and the business will not function in synchrony to achieve its goal.

Everyone must have proper expectations of the big ass goal before everyone sets out to make it happen. The last thing anyone would want for a business is to make it five years down the road and realize that nothing is driving the business forward, the goal is not as motivating as it needs to be and there are no clear action steps to implement a clear vision. All because the goal was built on false expectations or wrong measurements. **The business's goal can change, but the direction should always stay the same.** The carpenter may change his mind about what the final woodworking piece may look like, but he still needs to work with utmost precision, measurements, and communicate his expectations to everyone involved in the project so that the finished work turns out well.

I knew that "success" was the path I wanted to follow, so I created clear and specific action steps in that direction to ensure that success. "Success" in my mind was defined as a better life for my family, team members, community, and investments. Making a better life for family and team members is a highly motivating "WHY."

Dig deep introspectively to figure out exactly what you are working for and why, and let this help you create your big ass goal and action steps. We'll talk a little later about how to structure action steps to reach the big ass goal, but the first step is figuring out what your goal is and why. Measure twice, then enact the plan and appropriate action steps to cut the wood in the right direction.

Be sure your business has a clear "WHY" that is communicated clearly to everyone, supported with clear, measurable smaller action steps to get closer to fulfilling that "WHY" and accomplishing the big ass goal, *before* the business sets out on its course. **Save the business time and energy before ruining the product and wasting the cost, time, and energy put forth by you and the team members running head-strong into different directions with no trackable goal and an unclear motivation**. The wrong cut will be made by haphazard planning and leadership, and much more than a goal will be sacrificed by measuring once and cutting once.

Chapter 22 - Be a Piece of the Pie, Not the Knife that Cuts the Pie

As technology continues to advance, people fear being replaced by an automated computer, a better business, or a better system. This is a valid concern among people whose jobs truly can be replaced by an automated computer, self-checkouts, online stores, ATM machines, and more. The people who will be replaced are just tools in the transaction and tools are replaceable. These people are knives that cut the pie, not pieces of the pie. They are not vital points in the transaction or process and since they are not necessary, they should be replaced.

A good coach and cornerman are irreplaceable in the fighting world. Without a good coach and cornerman, the fighter won't be guided well to a win and the wheel to the fighting machine won't turn.

There are some jobs that only YOU as an individual can fulfill. Only YOU can be a good wife or husband to your spouse, only YOU can be a good daughter or son, sister, brother, mother or father to your family members, and only YOU can fulfill the purpose that God has for your life. Your job at the grocery store can be replaced with another grocery store worker. Your job at Starbucks can be replaced by another co-worker. But your job as an entrepreneur and team leader, business owner, coach, cornerman, or other leadership position is unique since you can make such an impact on your business that you may be considered irreplaceable. You can become so incredibly valuable to the business that if you were to leave, they may have to hire three people to replace the one job that you held as an instrumental piece to the business.

The people who will be replaced by machines and better businesses are not the first, the best, or the only in their business.

They are merely tools used to complete the transaction and are not essential parts to the transaction. The idea is to become a vital piece of the process so that you will not be replaced. If a mechanic breaks a wrench or other tool, he can easily get a new one. **But it is much harder to replace a good mechanic than it is to replace a tool.**

In real estate, people who just open doors and write contracts on preprinted paperwork will be replaced by machines or stellar agents. There is no expertise or professionalism in opening a door or filling out paperwork. Anyone can do that in their sleep. In real estate and other businesses, staff members must become a vital piece of the process in order to stand out in the client's mind.

How does someone become a vital piece of the process and not just a tool in the process? By bringing something to the table that cannot be done by a machine or anyone else. **By bringing wisdom and experience to the table. Becoming the expert.** Bringing the best interest of the client to the table and serving them with the highest degree of customer service. Bringing dedication to the community and service to various charities. Building their business on doing things that no one else wants or cares to do.

If your team truly works for the best interests of the clients, it will be made apparent to everyone that your team members are not just tools in the transaction, but pivotal pieces throughout the entire process.

It is so important to avoid contracting dirty sales breath in a transaction. Dirty sales breath decreases your trustworthiness with clients because you become more concerned about money and yourself rather than the best interests of your clients. **Encourage your team to keep the best interests of clients first, and this will ensure your team members remain vital pieces of the system.**

As a manager or business owner, it's important to treat
your employees as valuable pieces of the transaction, not just
tools in the transaction. Your employees make the wheel turn, so
tell them how important they are. My sales and administration staff
know that they are hyper-important to make sure our business runs
properly. They each have individual roles to fill, and if any of those
roles were not filled properly then our business would fail. They are
each vital to the team's success.

You must let your staff know their value. Do not keep
encouragement to yourself. If you think it, then recognize it by
saying it to others. Tell your staff and administrative personnel what
they mean to the business. **You need them and they need you, so
encourage them.** Be your team's motivation to succeed every day
and strive to be a piece of the pie, not a knife that cuts the pie.

Chapter 23 - Losses, Roadblocks and Wins

During my professional fighting career, whenever I won fights, I didn't want to remember the techniques that needed improvement upon in the fight. I only focused on the victory. But every time I lost a fight, I deconstructed the entire fight to the micro-details so that I could learn from the overall performance and improve for the future. I grew far more from a loss than I did from a victory.

I found myself in a winning streak and obliterated every opponent in the cage. In my pride I took a fight in a higher weight class and I got beat. Bad. I called my dad after the fight to let him know how the fight went, and I fully expected to hear the disappointment in his voice that would echo how I was feeling.

The first words he said when he answered the phone were: "It is ok..." I didn't have to tell him how badly I'd lost, he somehow already knew even though he didn't have a television and couldn't have found out before I called him. He continued, "It's ok, because if you never lose, you'll never know what it feels like to win."

I'd been so caught up in the numbers game of wins vs. losses that I wasn't challenging myself like I should have been. Dad was right, and I couldn't believe it took me this long to realize how important losses are for the ultimate win. When I had won in life, in sports, or in business, I hadn't learned anything. However, when I failed I learned what NOT to do and was more aware of my room for growth.

I also realized that if I couldn't disappoint my dad when I knew I was giving 100% of all my effort and strength, then I shouldn't be worried about disappointment at all – not with disappointing myself or others.

When we quit worrying about other people's expectations, then we quit worrying about our outcomes. And when we change our expectations, we change our outcomes.

When my fighters got nervous about my expectations for them before a fight, I made sure they understood that if they had trained as hard as they could and if they fought to win (even if they didn't actually win), then they would make the team proud. They knew they shouldn't walk into a fight expecting to win, but rather expecting to compete with themselves to challenge themselves. **This mindset prevents them from merely focusing on their losses or wins and challenges them to focus on their goals. This challenges them and changes their outcomes by changing their expectations.** When they quit worrying about winning vs. losing and start worrying about challenging themselves to promote their own self growth, they produce different results.

The same theory directly applies to the business world: when you challenge yourself and your business to grow from challenges instead of dwelling in self-pity from past failures, then you'll be amazed at the quick change in results. Your results change when your expectations change. The results that will be produced from your team's new outlook of self-growth as their priority vs. simply the idea of winning or losing will be much more profitable than previous results. **Keeping a self-growth outlook that is measurable, scalable, and sell-able and can produce measurable, scalable, and sell-able results.**

If you know anything about golf, you know that you must hit the golf-ball with the golf-club to make it in the hole...or at least get close. Every time you hit the ball but fail to make it in the hole, you are that much closer to the hole (in most cases). Although you fail by not hitting it in the hole, you win at the same time by hitting it closer to the hole, and you are also teaching yourself better technique, setting new goals for yourself, and improving your overall game through the putting process. Too many people give up because they get tired of the putting process - both in golf and in business.

Everyone is so scared of failure when failure is the true sign of growth.

There was a famous man who spent twenty-eight years filled with absolute failure before he gained his first major success. He is a prime example of what it looks like to persevere through failures, growing each time with measurable steps and achieving goals. In 1832 he lost his job and was defeated for state legislature. In 1833 he failed in his business. In 1835 the love of his life died. In 1836 he had a nervous breakdown and almost gave up on everything completely. In 1838 he was defeated for Speaker of the House. In 1843 he was defeated for nomination for Congress. In 1846 he was elected for Congress, but lost re-nomination in 1848. In 1849 He was rejected for land officer, defeated for U.S. Senate in 1854, defeated for nomination for Vice President and again for U.S. Senate in 1856 and 1858. Until FINALLY, in 1860, Abraham Lincoln was elected as U.S. President. **What looked like failing miserably for twenty-eight years was moral, emotional, and mental growth before he gained his first major success.**

Too often we get caught up in failure that we give up before the growth pays off. We forget that no one can score first place without failing first. No one remembers the person scoring second place, yet everyone must score second place before scoring first place. Sometimes we must go through twenty-eight years of absolute growth before that growth leads to a major success.

When I go on a business appointment and the client does not want to do business with me, I follow up with the client and ask what I can do to improve myself. I need feedback from my peers and my coach to learn where I am weak and improve on my weaknesses, so that I can learn from those losses and not let them hinder my future successes.

We have talked about failing vs. winning and focusing on self-growth instead of the fails and the wins, but I would like to talk a little about roadblocks along the way to success. Roadblocks are tricky since they can propel businesses forward by alternating the original plan to a new and improved plan, or they can truly set back a business if the business focuses on the obstacle.

When I was offered the job as a fighting instructor in Atlanta, it was hard to leave my home in Northeast Tennessee. I needed to expand my horizons but I had no idea where the good Lord was leading me. I made the transition to Georgia and it was hard. At the time I was making enough money from fighting and training to pay my rent and other bills, but every penny mattered. One thing led to another and I decided to shift my focus from fighting professionally to focus on instructing mixed martial arts. I was working for a gym in a small store-front that had a great program started and its business was continuing to increase... we all loved it! Until six months after I had started working at the gym, I went in to work one morning and there were chains on the door. The place had been completely locked up and shut down. I was shocked.

The owners were not paying the rent even though the business was making money. I couldn't believe it.

My wife had just left her business in northeast Tennessee to move to Georgia, so I had to fix this mess quickly since I had to bring in all the income for our family. At that time my only skill set was fighting, so I was at a loss for what else to do.

I texted all the contacts in my phone who had come to the gym letting them know that I would still teach private lessons in my garage until I could find a place to open my own gym. As it turned out, one of my buddies I had texted from the gym had an empty space in a strip mall available for rent and offered it to me for a good deal. I had some equipment that I had accumulated for the new gym location, we negotiated a good lease, and my wife and I decided to open our own gym. It took every bit of savings we had to open the doors of this new gym that we named, Moab Fighting Concepts. We had never done anything on our own like this, and it felt like we were stepping off a cliff. But we did it, and within one week we had business up and going again.

The failure of closing one location opened a door for us to move to a better location and opened a better opportunity for business in general. The chain on the door was not a roadblock. **Roadblocks only make people stumble on them if people focus on them. Just like losses. And just like wins.** If we focus on the losses, we'll stagger in self-pity. If we focus on the roadblocks, we'll stress and fail to develop a creative strategy to move around the roadblock or adapt our strategy because of them. If we focus on the wins, we will live with unreasonable expectations and lack of self-growth. **We must instead focus on promoting our own self-growth and using the setbacks to our advantage, challenging ourselves with measurable steps to reach our goals, regardless of the losses or wins.**

If you choose to bypass the roadblock in your path, then you can get to the better opportunity awaiting you after the roadblock. The Moab Fighting Concepts business has been profitable because we chose not to let that roadblock stop us from pushing forward. **If we all choose to persevere through failures and use them for our own self-growth, then the successes awaiting us are limitless.**

Your losses do not always mean you are weak or strong, and just because you may be strong in one area doesn't mean that you should ignore your weaknesses in another area. **When you persevere through failures you learn from your losses.**

Chapter 24 - Adapting, Reacting, and Pro-Acting

Have you ever had to present a plan to co-workers that wasn't received well and required many adaptations before implementation? Or when implementing a plan there arose a major conflict with someone that your original plan may not have accounted for? Whether we've had to adapt to last minute changes in our original plans or pro-actively work to avoid an issue with clients or co-workers, we've all been there and done that. Team leaders and entrepreneurs, business owners and other business executives may even have fun tallying up how many times a day they must adapt to hiccups in plans, and proactively work to solve problems among employees or clients.

As a leader, your ability to seamlessly adapt and react to any issues that may arise within the workplace, and then lead your team through them in a positive and constructive way, is vital to the growth and success of the team.

Fighters are trained to become extremely aware of their responses inside and outside of the ring, and must continually train their ability to adapt to a change in their strategy. They must train their minds to guess which move their opponent will make and proactively fight to keep their opponent from making that move.

Accustom yourself with what is happening in your team. You can prevent unforeseen issues by proactively thinking about where potential issues may arise and preparing yourself for the worst. **You can analyze how to resolve issues before they arise to save your business from greater loss.** When you coach the team to handle a potential hiccup before something bad actually happens, you help them see the bigger picture to figure out how to go around the roadblock. **Learn from your losses to be proactive in your business.**

You will have a better reaction or adaptation when you've already prepared yourself for the worst case scenario of any situation. **Reacting positively and always keeping the clients' best interests in mind fosters growth for the business, yet many team leaders focus on how their decisions will negatively affect themselves or their business without thinking first of their clients.**

If you focus on yourself before your clients, then you're building your business on sand. Even the Bible tells us that only idiots do that. People are smart and can transparently see through your motives. If you don't truly care about your clients, they won't want to do business with you. Hard times will allow others to see straight through you if you're not working proactively to prevent issues or are only focused on your own good when issues do arise. If your business focuses on serving your clients, you will have a better outlook for your business and your level of customer service will soar.

Customers only want to work with business people who will truly help them and work out the best for them. If you care more about yourself than them, they will see through your bullshit and you will have a much bigger issue on your hands than the one you were handling in the first place.

The key to adapting, reacting, and pro-acting is the ability to remove yourself from the immediate situation and look at everything from a 30,000-foot view, calm down and avoid stressing over the situation, ask questions to all parties involved to find out what the solution should be from their perspective, and then communicate clearly to all parties what needs to happen to solve the issue appropriately based on their responses.

Practice handling objections and crises with your team daily. Have fun role playing and scripting to train your team members how to prepare for any unexpected conflict. Training them to remove themselves from the immediate situation and look at all the details from a big-picture perspective is the first step. Responding out of impulse or anger is NEVER an option, since all team members should keep the client's interests as their top priority. Seeking a solution from a level of service is an important reaction and adaption to any situation. Teaching your team to prepare for the worst by role playing objections trains them to think on the spot for solutions to problems. If thinking on the spot is not a strength of anyone on your team, then practice. Hire a coach to help your team learn. Ask an executive to provide more training in this area to your team, but enact this in your business and your level of service will be greatly improved.

Chapter 25 - Discipline is Everything

In any situation I will always pass up an opportunity learning from the smartest guy in the room to learn from the guy who wants the most to become the best and become the smartest. For **he is the hardest worker in the room, and he will become the best and the smartest. Not by raw talent, but by discipline and dedicated desire.**

I have seen unathletic athletes and fighters become far advanced in their sport because of their regimented diet, coaches, systematic training, persistent dedication, consistent goal-setting, and trained talent. I have seen raw talent loose horribly to the unathletic hard worker. **Hard work and discipline beats talent every time.**

Discipline is everything. I could easily leave the whole chapter as just those three words. Discipline. Is. Everything. If we do not keep a strong mindset, high discipline, and will-power in our lives then it will be impossible for us to succeed in anything. People who lack discipline will forever be stuck feeling sorry for themselves. Those people have not yet learned the behavior of keeping a disciplined mindset. Hell will freeze over before they will take the first step toward showing initiative and discipline, because they are comfortable where they are.

Anything you can improve upon is a learned behavior, and you can improve any behavior with time, coaching and consistent discipline.

If you have discipline, or think you have discipline, test yourself. Do you think you are a hard worker? I challenge you to wake up two hours earlier every day. In those two hours I challenge you to do an intensive exercise, work a second job, start a project for the community, learn another language, or spend those two hours furthering your education in an area where you are interested. Discipline yourself to this routine for six months. If you are already getting up at four o'clock in the morning or earlier, I challenge you to work this extra time into your schedule when you are able.

This discipline challenge will not only strengthen your will-power to succeed with more determination in your morning schedule to win the first round of your day, but you'll magically see stronger discipline appear in your work and family life.

When you increase discipline in one area of your life, it will increase in all other areas of life. When you slack off in one area of life, your discipline will automatically lack in all areas of life. Put the discipline and accountability in place to do what you may not want to do, and what you are currently not doing, for six months.

If you choose not to do this challenge, realize that someone else is doing it. Someone else is more disciplined than you and wants success more than you do, so they will get the win before you do. If you are alright with this then you don't want success for your business, yourself, or your family badly enough and may not yet have what it takes to push yourself to the next level. You are the one who needs to hold yourself accountable to this six-month challenge more than anyone else.

If you do not feel self-motivated enough to do this, then it's time to stop complaining. Plan the habits, routine and precise schedule for your days and weeks, and if you stay consistently a slave to your schedule then you do not need motivation. This discipline and consistency will become such a strong habit of routine you won't even think twice when the alarm rings at 3:59am and you'll naturally train yourself to be out of the bed by four o'clock, no excuses or complaints. Hold yourself accountable to this routine or have someone else hold you to it if you want to add a layer of accountability. **Determine today that you will remain disciplined when others fail to be disciplined**. You can do it. You are the champion, so take control of your mornings, your days, your weeks, your life by increasing your discipline now to build success.

Success requires boundaries and boundaries require discipline. You must take care of business now to succeed later. Set the boundaries you need to make what you need happen. **Take care of your business first, since the type of life you want to give your family comes first**. Have the discipline to work long hours and put your nose to the grindstone. **Overwork yourself now so that you will have more time and resources to lavish on your family later.** Some may disagree with me on this, but you must always and firmly do what you must to live out your beliefs and attain your goals, even if that means working long hours at first to spend more time with your family later. Do what you must to provide for your family above all if that is your motivator.

Decide what your boundaries and goals are, then keep them. What motivates you? Find out what it is, then work with discipline to do it. Fight for the win.

Chapter 26 - Study Up to Level Up

It was his first time competing. I could tell he was getting nervous and understandably so, since it was his first fight. I had trained my pro-fighter well and he was prepared to win his first fight whether he thought he could. Dustin stood across from his first opponent and I could tell he needed a quick pep-talk. I pulled him aside and said, "I want you to look at that guy. He's half the size that I am. There's no way that this guy can hit you nearly as hard as you've been hit in training."

He nodded. He understood that if he could take a hard punch in the face by me, 210 pounds of mean muscle at the time, then fighting another man who weighed 150 pounds would be a piece of cake.

Now he could get through the fight and win since his perspective was adjusted. His opponent didn't seem as daunting after he checked his perspective and gained confidence.

Dustin had been training with someone who was better, bigger, and could hit harder than this opponent. He'd trained with a more experienced fighter and it caused him to level up in the fight, recognize his advantage, and gain confidence.

If you train hard to strive to be the best that you can be, then all obstacles become small. If an obstacle isn't small, then you haven't trained or educated yourself enough, or you lack the confidence needed to succeed.

Any time you train at a high level, the smaller the obstacles become. This is the reason you must continue to self-educate yourself and your team. **When you study up, you level up. When you level up, you gain confidence and dominate. It starts with training harder than everyone else and keeping the perspective**

that since you have trained harder than anyone else, you can handle more obstacles that seem too big for everyone else.

Let's say I am working my first day in the real estate business and I've never had to handle an objection before. Then a seller tells me, "I don't want to work with you, I want to work with another agent." This seems like the biggest obstacle in the world to overcome! It can be assumed that I wouldn't know how to seamlessly handle rejection or objection on the first day of a job.

But, say it was the first day on the job and I didn't know anything else besides my new team's mission and vision, and I truly believed that my team was the best in the business because my boss had done a great job showing me why the business does what it does for its clients. If I truly believed that I was being trained by the best and that those surrounding me in the business were the best, then I would have the confidence needed to handle that objection or rejection. I would believe that the service I could provide would be better than any other in the business. It would be a piece of cake to market myself to that client if I checked my perspective and had confidence.

If you believe in yourself and your business, you will be unstoppable. Confidence can defeat any objection or rejection. When you train with those who are better than you, then what was once an objection is not actually an objection anymore. Now you can conquer that objection with confidence. **Train up to level up and you will have unbeatable confidence to succeed.**

Confidence is similar to discipline. If you lack confidence in one area of life, you'll lack confidence in other areas of life. If you believe in your business and are confident in your services, confident in your ability to succeed because of your hard work and discipline, confident in yourself, then you won't care what anyone else thinks. You will not feel self-conscious. You will be free from feeling "not good enough." You will stop believing lies and confidently believe the truth that you are the first, the best, and the only one in your business who can succeed and serve at a higher level than anyone else.

Study up to level up. Gain the training you need to be confident in your belief that you and your team are the best in your field of business. Do what other businesses don't want to do so that you can become the expert, then be confident in the fact that *you are the expert*. **When you gain this level of confidence, you'll be able to handle any objection or opponent since no one else will come close to the level of training and experience that you have gained.**

Chapter 27 - Death by Mediocrity

I trained with many good fighters who were well-trained. Even though they were well-trained, they didn't challenge themselves as best as I thought they could - which didn't necessarily make them any less of a good fighter - I just had higher expectations for them than what they had for themselves. They could have challenged themselves harder, but they did not since they did not have high enough expectations for themselves.

My mission of training hard and fighting was to test myself as an athlete past the limits I had set for myself. I wanted to see how far I could push myself mentally, physically, and emotionally past my breaking points. A lot of people failed to push themselves harder for the sake of keeping a good fighting record. They wanted to stay undefeated or pad their record, so they stayed comfortable and didn't push themselves further since they weren't hungry enough for success.

My team and I fought wherever and whenever we could, no matter how short-notice or how far in advance the fight had been planned, we fought anytime. We fought in higher weight-classes. We trained longer days. Held stricter diets. This allowed us never to settle for mediocrity. We did not want to be the best in our skill level, but we wanted to push ourselves so that we could be the best of the higher skill level.

We are the only ones who set limits on ourselves, allowing us to serve as our own worst enemy and our own best motivator.

As a business leader, it is your job to push the limits of the business. As a team leader or business owner, you cannot let your team settle for mediocrity. All the sales and administration staff under you must understand how important it is for the business never to settle for mediocrity. **The moment someone starts settling for mediocrity is the moment the business decreases in production and service**. Your constant goal should always be to save your business from the loss of money and opportunity that come with mediocrity.

It is important to push every limit, every day, for the business and your staff. **Push forward for market share to show your staff that the business is hungry for growth. Encourage your team to grow so that your team can reap the benefits**. Your team, no matter how large, is like your family and depends on the business just like your own family depends on you. You must keep their needs before your own. **Grow the business to bless your team. Grow the business to show the market that you dominate in production and service.**

Strive to feed your team better. **Don't settle for less than the best along the way, believe that you can always do better.** Encourage your team to exceed their expectations and hold one another to a greater standard of service and work. As iron sharpens iron, when you all work to be the best that you can be and more, the business will be known for the highest level of service and will soon be best in the business. **Kill any ounce of mediocrity in the business and replace it with excellence.**

Chapter 28 - Pulling the Sled

Have you noticed that in retail and food service jobs, the hardest worker ends up doing all the work and maintaining the most responsibility even if they're still getting paid the same as everyone else? They end up pulling everyone else's weight and consequently do not last long in their position before their burnout gets the best of them and they quit. The same is true in any group project, there is usually one person who ends up doing most of the work and by the end of the project, this person hates everyone else and everything about the project since they basically did it all themselves. Interesting, isn't it? There are some people who just love doing all the work because they are very hard working, task-oriented with a type A personality, and think that they are the only ones able to do the job well enough. I was this person for a long time. I have these people working in my businesses, and they know who they are.

Although the world would not function without type A personality people, it is important that these people are careful not to take the full load on their shoulders in your business, or they will experience burnout too quickly. Oh, does this describe you? And are you in a leadership position? It is even more important that you do NOT try to take the whole weight of the business on your shoulders, you will fail to handle it as well as those around you who are paid to own their positions of the business. It is important that you let those around you do their jobs without your micromanagement. They will do it better than you and are getting paid to do it better than you, so trust them to do so. We'll talk about this a little later in the book when we talk about the importance of macro-management over micro-management, so stay tuned.

The most successful fighters have learned that they need a strong team of people surrounding them to train, coach, encourage, and work beside everyday. They understand that they can't fight alone. Left on their own, they wouldn't be half the fighter they are today without their support team.

A fool is a man trying to pull his sled up the mountain by himself when he has a team of huskies eager and able to help him. **Likewise, a fool is a man who is trying to single handedly pull the weight of the business by himself when he has a team of hard workers eager and willing to share the workload and help pull the weight.**

If you can ensure that your team members are in correct positions in the business to pull the appropriate weight of the business, then you'll have a well working machine.

As a business owner or team leader, if you can get 100% buy-in with your staff when implementing a system or transaction, then you win. **If you can get everyone on board with the same vision and if everyone understands the "why" behind the business, then you can better distribute the weight and work of the business.** Instead of prying ten people to do what you want them to do, work on getting them on board with your "why." When people are on the same page and share the same vision, now you have ten people plus yourself pushing towards the same goal, instead of just yourself pushing toward a goal, while also pushing ten people to do what you need them to do. You have a whole team to boost your business to the next level and hold one another accountable to the goal. Now the whole team understands and can explain the "why" to others who may not get it. Now you are not single handedly trying to pull the sled up the mountain. You have a team of huskies working together.

You need the right goals and systems to help your team as they all work to pull the heavy sled. If you don't have all the working roles and parts, then things will quickly fall apart and slide down the mountain. Think of ways to benefit and invest in your team. Let them know how important they are for the business. You couldn't carry the weight or pull the sled without them, so make sure they're treated well. Don't try fighting alone for the win.

Staff loyalty is built when your team truly matters to you, their voice is heard, and their opinion matters. Along with guaranteeing that your staff is loyally on board with the vision of the business and are working together to pull the sled, each staff member must be receiving the pay they deserve.

I hate it when I a real estate agent hire an administrative staff and after three months when the admin leaves, the agent throws a fit. When all the while the agent had refused to pay the admin above minimum wage. Unfortunately, this happens often especially in my industry and area.

If you want loyal staff who are high producing, then you cannot pay them the same as starter employees. You cannot pay them minimum wage. **If you cannot afford to pay someone what they are worth, then hire someone else. Or else you won't win their loyalty.** You'll spend all your time creating systems and procedures for this person and then they will leave because they cannot afford to live on the income you're providing.

Run your business right. Pay people what they're worth.

My biggest pet peeve is hearing people say, "I was going to leave my position for a better praying job, but then my boss offered me an opportunity I couldn't pass up." If someone is worth what their boss is just now offering to pay them, then why wasn't their boss paying them that amount the entire time? The boss was pocketing extra money from that employee since they did not truly value that employee's worth.

I understand that in some instances managers cannot pay their staff their deserved salary in the beginning of the business, perhaps because of start-up fees or other regulations along those lines. In these cases, it is the manager's responsibility to find ways to supplement the pay that their employee is unable to take home. **Take care of the people who take care of you.**

Eventually your team members and their hard work will be all that you are depending for your business, so it is important to be wise and ethical by paying people what they are worth.

If you fail to communicate that your employees' time and work are valuable, then they're wasting their time working for you. If you steal their time away from another job where they could be making what they deserve, then you are doing them a disfavor by hiring them in the first place. **Pay your staff what they deserve, or you will quickly lose their loyalty and may be left to pull the sled alone.** This would leave you a fool, so pro-actively avoid this issue now by appropriately paying your staff members what they need for the positions they maintain in your business.

Chapter 29 - Aim Small; Miss Small

Bill Morris. A man who kept me out of trouble growing up, and truly wanted the best for me. He not only wanted to see me live a life for God and succeed in business, but he invested his time into training me as a child how to be a good man and how to hunt. He taught me how to shoot a bow and arrow as he himself was an excellent archer. But he didn't stop there. He taught be how to *make* the bows and *make* the arrows, and then to hunt with them.

I remember one time we were shooting and even though I'd been practicing, I couldn't aim nearly as good as he could. He turned to me and said, "Son, your problem is that you're just aimin' for the target. When you aim for the target, you're just hittin' the target. You need to start aimin' for the bullseye, and you'll start hittin' the bullseye." He always hit the bullseye because he always aimed at the bullseye. His lesson to me was that if I aimed small, I missed small. If I aimed at the bullseye and barely missed, I was closer than if I aimed at the target and missed the bullseye by a long shot. I had to narrow my actions to meet my goal.

What a great business lesson in setting smaller action steps to help attain your big ass goal. If you aim small, you will miss small. You can achieve your big ass goal by creating specific and trackable actions to hone in on the outcome you want to attain.

Anyone who has shot a gun before also understands this. If you want to hit the barn, you hit the barn. Good. There was no challenge, and no way of measuring your skill or challenging your potential. Let's say that you have a big ass goal of becoming the world champion of hitting 5,000 bullseyes in one and a half hours. The action steps or "sub-goals" to achieve this big ass goal require first gaining the ability to hit bullseyes, and challenging yourself with narrow, specific steps to reach your seemingly *UN*attainable goal. If you narrow your first action step to shooting at the bullseye on the barn, which is more specific than just the building, now you can put forth the procedures and measure your progress with this smaller action to attain your big ass goal of hitting 5,000 bullseyes in 1.5 hours. You know what it'll take to put everything in place to hit your narrowed, specific bullseye so that you can attain your big ass goal.

A goal is not "I want to do all that I can do!" That is trash. It is not measurable or specific and it will not challenge you. There is no accountability in a vague statement like that. However, if you make your big ass goal specific: "This year I want to complete 250 transactions with my team and hit nearly $2 million in gross commission income for the team." Then you break this specific goal down to measurable "sub-goals" or action steps. For instance, "I will reach this goal by building the success of my team through more education, more efficient systems, and better policies and procedures to maintain twenty contracts or more each month."

A goal not set is a goal not hit. You must start setting goals to move yourself and your business anywhere. When you make and reach your goals, you unlock the potential to breakthrough to the next level.

You cannot grow what you do not track. It is necessary to strategically plan to meet these goals by breaking the big ass goal down into big action steps or "sub-goals." Set one big ass goal, then have three "sub-goals" that must be met in order to even come close to hitting your original goal. Then break those three "sub-goals" down further into five smaller steps to ensure that each "sub-goal" is met. This allows you to avoid feeling daunted by the weight of the big ass goal. If you focus on the "sub-goals" you will just have to meet the fifteen small tasks to come close to reaching the big ass goal. Focus one bite at a time to eat the whole elephant. If you get those fifteen tasks done, the big ass goal takes care of itself and who knows, you might just achieve what you never thought was possible.

Don't worry about your dollars. Worry about your pennies and your dollars will take care of themselves.

It is important to know who you are and where you're strong, but it is even more important to know where you are NOT strong. This will help you reach your goals. Knowing where you are strong will not help you nearly as much as recognizing where you are weak. When you recognize where you are weak then you can be held accountable for growth in those areas. **When you are coached, held accountable, self-educated, and driven to meet your tasks, then you will do all that it takes to grow in your weaknesses and continue in your strengths to complete each task until all the sub goals are met.** Then you'll hit the bullseye.

Goal tracking is the life blood of any business. If you do not track it, you cannot grow it and if you cannot grow it, then you cannot control it.

We track everything so minutely that I can tell exactly where we need to correct things and why. Even if the issue is so miniscule that only a magnifying glass could catch it. Tracking like this shows me immediately when we are headed off target and need to correct our trajectory before we slide any farther off course. Tracking goals also allows me to coach and mentor the team, hold them accountable, and put their goals into perspective. I have weekly one-on-one meetings with my staff so that I can hold them accountable to their own game plan and reassess goals if we need to. **If I don't hold them accountable to their goals, it is a failure on my end since I would be communicating to my team that I don't care enough about their success to hold them accountable to achieving it.**

Let's say one of my agents tells me that their goal for the month is to obtain four new deals under contract. I see from tracking their productivity that when the agent calls twenty people, they get two appointments, and they need four appointments for one under contract or sold. Tracking their progress allows me to tell them they will need to make one hundred and sixty calls to gain sixteen appointments, to gain four new deals under contract. That goal is now trackable. Attainable. Specific. Scalable and sell-able. This smaller action step helps the team with their big ass goal of 250 transactions for the year.

Your #1 priority for your team and your business should be helping them succeed. Take the time to sit down with each of them one-on-one and help them write out a big ass goal with three "sub-goals" and five smaller tasks under each "sub-goal." Track their progress and track their goals. Encourage them. Challenge them. Help them succeed and hit the bullseye by aiming small to achieve the impossible.

Chapter 30 - Hiring Puzzle Pieces

The biggest and ugliest challenge as a business leader (or owner) is to find the perfect puzzle pieces to fit into your business to build the perfect puzzle. As a leader, you must understand that each person you interview is a perfect fit to *a* puzzle, even if they don't fit into *your* puzzle.

Although failure is inevitable, failure because of a bad hire can be detrimental. Failure is important for growth as previously discussed, but it can also send a business reeling backward if the business isn't careful. Failure can be compared to a trampoline – sometimes it is necessary to fall backward in order to catapult forward at a higher speed.

Failure due to a poor decision in the hiring process can be a cancer for your culture.

The business you've created becomes a family as they build rapport and trust each other. Bringing the wrong puzzle piece into your culture can poison the culture and will take a long time to get out of the system. **BE SLOW TO HIRE and quick to fire.**

As a leader, you must also be an encourager to your team. Encourage your puzzle pieces in the position where they fit, for they should fit that position perfectly. Encourage your puzzle pieces to move into another position if you see that another position would better fit them.

Focus on your strengths and hire your weaknesses. In doing this, where you are weak someone else is strong. I'm a driver and "go-getter," so I hired someone who was more detailed and system oriented than me to help forward the business. This caused the business puzzle to look like a "go-getter" with organization. If you are already a very organized person, then your first hire should be a very loyal driver who can conquer the day and understand the hustle. Hire different personality types to make your puzzle more colorful and advantageous for the business.

Your team needs a variety of personality types with various strengths and weaknesses in order to fit together as a puzzle. Familiarize yourself with the various personality profiles. Learn to recognize them in others. **No one can make a puzzle out of just corner pieces, so don't try building your business with just one type of personality or profile.**

The DISC personality profile measures four quadrants of your behavioral style, preferences, and personality tendencies:

• Decisiveness — demonstrated in a team member who shows a high knack for problem solving and attaining results.

• Interactiveness — demonstrated in a team member who prefers interacting with others and exhibiting emotions while getting the job done as a team.

• Stability — demonstrated in a team member with a great ability for pacing, persistence, and consistency.

• Cautiousness — demonstrated in a team member who thrives in procedures, standards, and protocols.

On my real estate team, my buyer's agents need to score a high "Decisiveness" or a high "Interactiveness" level on the DISC profile to show clients properties in the spur of the moment and challenge themselves to make the phone calls necessary. They understand that phone calls = clients = under contract = sold homes = happy clients.

The listing agents need to have very good communication skills and score a high "Cautiousness" or high "Stability" level on the profile so that they can implement good systems for keeping track of all the details. My listing manager needs to be obsessive over all systems and communications.

My client care manager needs to be a nurturer scoring a high "Interactiveness" or high "Stability" level on the profile, helping people feel satisfied as they cross the finish line and cultivate relationships along the way with a familiar and warm personality.

The lead admin and office manager must be super detail-oriented scoring a high "Cautiousness" level, able to implement and enforce procedures to improve efficiency in systems when necessary.

It is important that you keep a list of non-negotiables for new hires to exhibit if you want to avoid making an incorrect hire. For instance, the non-negotiables for my team are as follows: the new hire must have the same moral beliefs as me and the team. The new hire should want to do what is right for other people even if it gives the new hire no benefit for themselves. Any new hire must have a high work ethic and strive to be the hardest worker in the room. The new hire must be coachable and able to see that there is a paved path already made for them to walk along, they should not re-create the wheel until they are successful in the position that they fulfill.

Complete your due diligence with future employees to make sure that they have the same moral beliefs, are coachable, and will follow your systems and procedures. Make sure they will do things the way your team has done them or needs them to be done. Communicate as their leader how important it is to for them to learn the tried and true until they master the existing road map of the business, and then they can have the freedom to be creative within appropriate boundaries and take ownership of their position. They should not start their first day on the job and try to change all the current systems of the business.

Years ago, some of the fighters I coached each wanted to create a technique and style of fighting that had never been exercised before. Instead of focusing on the core principles of Jiu jitsu, kickboxing and wrestling that are tried and true, they wanted to create their own path. **Because they were so focused on trying to do something no one else had done before, they lost out on several opportunities to excel in the tried and true techniques that they already knew**. Instead of following the path that had already been created by thousands of years in combat sports, they tried to reinvent the wheel, and it cost them victories in the long-run.

There is a road map given to your new hires by the people who have gone before them. Everyone naturally wants to assume that they are smarter than everyone else. So as young entrepreneurs and business people, your new hires may want to do things their way instead of following the tried and true path...they should not be allowed to do this until they become successful in the position they are meant to fill. **We all must be reminded to focus on mastering the principles of business - no matter what we are doing - that have already been created before us**, or else we risk wasting our resources and effort because of our pride.

Your new hires should know how the wheel works before they start changing its tread.

Each new hire should contribute to the team's positive outlook and challenge other team members to continue meeting goals. If someone isn't positive in their outlook, they will inevitably fail in the business because their outlook will become a self-fulfilling prophecy. If someone keeps a positive outlook and contributes to a positive team morale, then everyone in the team will benefit and be built up.

If someone has a negative outlook, then they will always have negative results. It is hard to keep accountability with people who think and act negatively. You cannot tell people with negative outlooks that the way they look at life is a direct result of how they think, because they won't want to believe you. **When you change your expectations you can change your outlook. When you change your outlook you change your results.**

If you want them to change their outlook, change yours. Any team member cannot listen to a leader they cannot respect. **As a leader, you must earn their respect just like the new hire should earn your respect.** Teach your team to find a positive outlook and perspective in everything. Ignore the negative. Compartmentalize and do not let negativity seep into the team culture. There is always something positive to be found in anything, and you set the pace for the team to recognize this.

Let's say that you have $100,000 in your bank account. Someone steals $800 from you. Would you rather spend the rest of your money, all $99,200 in finding the person who took the $800 and suing them to return it to you? Or would you let the lost money go? Now think of the dollars in terms of minutes in your life.

Your life is too precious to waste on negativity. Too precious to waste in worry, arguments, conflict, and the like. Ignore the negative. Let it go. Focus on the positive. Do not waste your limited moments on negativity. Instead, focus on making sure that the puzzle pieces of your business are receiving what they need and keeping a positive outlook for the health of the business.

Chapter 31 - Nearsighted and Farsighted Game Plans

Some people choose to live a healthy lifestyle now so that they can enjoy the benefits later in life that come from keeping a healthy lifestyle today. If you choose not to live a healthy lifestyle today, then although it may seem like you are living life to the fullest with beer, pizza, and ice cream every night without any exercise, you will pay the price down the road. **If you choose not to think ahead and plan now for long-term results, then your decisions made now will hurt you down the road.**

No successful fighter dreamt to be a world class champion but lacked the short-term decision making skills to accomplish their long-term goal. Every successful fighter understands both near and farsighted game plans.

You may have short-term goals to keep a healthy lifestyle, but if you don't understand the meaning of the long-term goal for keeping a healthy lifestyle, then the short-term goals may become less important overtime and harder to keep as you lose sight of the long-term goal. **This is an example of short-sighted tendencies that blind the ability to see the bigger picture**. Or, you could be so focused on the long-term goal that you never allow yourself a break, and it is a massive struggle to meet the short-term goals needed to bring the long-term goal into fruition. **This is an example of a global perspective that lacks the ability to keep short term goals.** We all fall somewhere on the spectrum.

The same theory applies to playing a game of checkers. What may seem like a good move now, without thinking ahead, may lead to your defeat in the game a few moves later. If you strategize to think of the bigger picture, then you may decide to make a different move now to lead to your overall victory in the game.

You will inevitably have nearsighted people and farsighted people working together on your team. This can both help and hurt your team at the same time. The possible benefits to this combination are that the farsighted goal focusers will help the nearsighted goal focusers see the overall future game plan and keep them motivated in the everyday details and short-term goals. Just like the nearsighted goal focusers will help the farsighted goal focusers see the details that need to be done along the way to bring the long-term goals to fruition. Both can help each other if they're working together properly.

Those who cannot see through the nearsighted goal lens cannot train their brain to understand how the details and short-term goals will move the team from here to there. They just think globally to create BIG plans with BIG ideas, but have a hard time implementing them. **These people are mostly farsighted thinkers who contribute well to the team but may never be able to see the importance in the details**. Details may overwhelm them, or they may think of the short-term goals as unnecessary.

Ask questions to lead these big-picture thinkers to envision growth for the company and then listen to their input. Place them in positions for the team where they do not have to be bogged down in the short-term details or goals, but can help the team create farsighted goals, big ideas for growth, and future plans. **Pair these people with nearsighted thinkers to help them implement their big picture plans, and in doing so, you'll also help the short-term goal oriented people see the bigger picture.** This dynamic duo may help the farsighted thinkers recognize the importance of the nearsighted goals and details.

People who are too short-term goal oriented are too nearsighted in their thinking to see the bigger picture. **They do not have to fully understand the long-term goals, but they must at least believe in the same goal and vision of the team. Or else they**

are cancerous to the team. These team members MUST understand the importance of the long-term goals, or else their loyalty will falter since they are not fully on board with the business's or team's goals.

If people cannot understand the farsighted goals, then explain the short-term goals VERY well to them. They may not understand the long-term goal no matter how many times you slap them sideways to make them understand it. They are nearsighted in their understanding, and most likely just worrying about today's problems without planning for the future. **For these people, they will not understand the farsighted goals and you must help them understand the short-term vision and goals that feed into the farsighted goals, vision, and ultimate game plan**. Or prepare for them to quit since they cannot grasp why the business does what it does, where the team or business is going, and how it will meet its goals.

If your team members do not understand the business's short-term or long-term goals, like poison it will deteriorate their customer service, their perseverance, work ethic, ambition, discipline, and attitude. Like a disease this will spread to other team members. Soon you'll have an anarchy if you fail to build the team with individuals who understand the team's overall vision (even if they do not fully understand certain aspects).

Neither type of personality is bad for the business since both personalities help the other where they are weak, so use this to your advantage by pairing the farsighted thinkers with the detail oriented, nearsighted thinkers to help each other excel and further understand the team's overall vision.

Chapter 32 - Holding the Shepherd Staff

As sheep know the voice of their shepherd, your team must trust your leadership and voice. As their leader, you hold the shepherd's staff and must lead them responsibly. Hold the team strictly accountable to the rules. If you hold everyone accountable, there won't be a lot of conflict. They will know that you care about them when you keep them disciplined. **You cannot lead with an iron fist, but you must be regimented and consistent with your instruction, coaching, and direction. The team must believe that you will fight for them. Love them by holding them accountable to the strict expectations.**

When I was fighting, my coach held high expectations for me and told me that an **expectation with no consequence is an idea.** It isn't an expectation if it isn't enforced. There were consequences for expectations not met, and rewards for expectations exceeded.

It is important to reward your team members when they reach their goals. Help them track their progress, challenge them, then celebrate with them when they accomplish what they thought they could not. In the same manner, if an employee arrives to office three minutes late after clear expectations have been set for a timely arrival to the office, send the employee back home for the day. Tell them they are not needed since they were needed on time or not at all. Sounds strict? Maybe. Sounds black and white? YES. That employee will never be late again. There must be consequences for expectations set, no matter the relationship you have with your employees. Treat everyone the same, completely equal in all regards.

You should not allow the team any room for gray areas or confusion, conflict, or slacking. You should strictly hold to black and white categories only. Build your policies and procedures to be black and white with no gray area. This will also diminish any amount of conflict that may arise within the team. When there is conflict, someone is right and the other person is wrong. **It is just overall easier to decipher the course of action for the team when everything is black and white.** Anytime gray area does sneak its way in, you should always err on the side of the best interests for the team and business, not your own.

A good leader not only leads by enforcing the set expectations, but also leads by asking questions to further growth in all team members. A great book that dives into further details about this is called *The Coaching Habit* by Michael Stanier which describes such an excellent approach to leadership.

Educate your employees to analyze, think and create their own solutions to their own problems. Sometimes you must educate them to see the right solution and sometimes you must change their vision and outlook to allow them to see the right way themselves. Once they change their outlook, they become part of the answer to their problem's solution. They aren't just someone implementing someone else's plan or doing something a certain way because they were told to do so...they become part of the problem's solution and will take ownership both over the issue and what it takes to resolve it. Asking questions leads to further growth within the team.

As the leader in charge, you are responsible for managing well in an honest and trustworthy fashion. Act professional and appropriate around your personnel, and think before you speak to filter out any inappropriate comment or gesture in your interactions with others. Lead by example. Follow the safety procedures and know the rules and guidelines of the company so that you can ensure your cooperation. Show others how and why they need to comply with the black and white expectations of the team.

If an employee scheduled a meeting with a client and the employee had to cancel for whatever reason, then you need to step up to the plate and take the appointment yourself. Make sure that you know how to function in any position of the business and have the humility to fill in at the drop of a hat if an employee does not show up to work, quits, or heaven forbid, dies unexpectedly. **Leading from example shows others that you can be trusted and that you understand what they are experiencing. You hold the shepherd's staff, so handle it appropriately.**

Chapter 33 - No bad Staff, Only Bad Leaders

As a leader you must accept all responsibility for everything bad that happens in your office, on your team, and within your business. You oversee the hiring and the firing processes. You oversee providing all the training in between. **If someone is a bad fit for a position, then you made a mistake by hiring that person and not firing that person. You blundered by failing to provide the training that person needs to fulfill that position correctly.** You miscommunicated expectations or failed to provide clear enough instruction. **A true leader controls what comes in and what comes out and takes responsibility for all the difficult and complicated shit that comes with it.** That is why it is so important to hire slow and fire fast.

If a client calls you with a complaint about the office staff or team member, the very first thing you should do is genuinely apologize. No matter how hard it is for you to bite your tongue. Listen well to the client and then take all the responsibility for the issue since YOU (and NO ONE ELSE) are fully in charge of the hiring, training, and firing processes. You control everything that would make your agents, team members, or employees succeed or fail. So YOU are the one who must take responsibility when things go south. **Even when the client's opinion is incorrect, it is important to handle their opinion in the most appropriate way with the highest level of service.** You don't have to agree with the client to serve them well. In fact, no one believes that they are wrong, and the client is clearly feeling discontent for a reason. Your job is to affirm the client, apologize, and make it right.

If you have supervisors that you report to, then YOU (and NO ONE ELSE) is responsible for any shit that hits the fan. Even if a new hire appears to be 100% responsible for a transaction gone wrong, you are ultimately responsible since you failed to correctly train them or communicate expectations. So you are the one who needs to apologize to your supervisors on behalf of the situation for your lack of oversight.

You are their coach for their fight, so take ownership of the whole fight – the good, the bad, and the ugly. **Train them after you eat the sin and take full ownership for the thing that went wrong.** Then approach your staff in a way that empowers them and helps them learn from the experience. Leaders must accept COMPLETE ownership for anything that happens. I cannot stress this enough.

All experience is not good experience, but you want to make sure that the teaching experience is something your team wants to repeat. When there is a lesson to be learned you must teach it with grace and wisdom so that they can be well equipped to handle the same situation better in the future.

Remember when anything is BAD, it is the team LEADER'S fault. When anything is GOOD, it is the TEAM who receives the credit. They're the ones bringing in the clients, and they're the ones who need to make sure they get all the credit for the good praise.

If you are interested in a more in-depth motivation on this topic, *The Dichotomy of Leadership* by Jacko Willink and Leif Babin, is a highly recommended resource for you to add to your library.

Chapter 34 - Disciplinary vs. Friendly

In order to show love, you must show discipline. A parent wants to be their children's friend, and sometimes they feel like if they discipline their children they will lose the status of a "friend." I argue that children have enough friends and they don't need their parents to be their friends. They need their parents to be parents. Discipline and love work together to form a consistent and authoritative leadership that children need and even crave, and this combination is essential to the child's development. If the child receives more discipline than love, then the child is more likely to feel overpowered and unloved, often resulting in bitterness toward the parents. If the child feels more love than discipline, then the child is more likely to feel like they are permitted to do anything they want to without any negative consequence. If both love and discipline are lacking, then the child most likely feels neglected or abandoned. The balance of love and discipline create a trusting relationship between the child and parents and communicates clear expectations, consistent discipline when necessary, plenty of love, safety, responsiveness and support to the child. The same authoritative leadership format applies well to business.

In my very first management position I was faced with a decision to fire a close friend. I was mentally and emotionally upset with him and distraught in my position as his boss and his friend. But I had to make the decision. I had to take a minute to compartmentalize business with business and life with life. In this moment, he needed me as his manager to show disciplinary action and teach him a life lesson. But later, he needed a loving friend to encourage him in his strengths. So I fired him.

After I fired him, he asked me, "Are we still going to meet tonight for dinner?" and my response was, "Of course, see you there." Nothing else was ever said about the situation. From then on, our relationship stayed the same and nothing changed even though I had fired him. It is so important to compartmentalize business with business and life with life, being both a friend when necessary and a disciplinary when necessary. Too many leaders take situations too personally, unfortunately, and that prevents them from doing this well. **You must work to compartmentalize work and life; separate the two and keep them separate.**

It is important to be ready at anytime to show discipline to anyone when the situation requires a disciplinary action. Even if the employee is a dear friend. **If you fail to show discipline when the situation arises, then team members will not revere you as the leader they need. If you fail to show love when needed, employees may feel too overpowered and unimportant, and not revere you as the leader they need.** They need and crave an authoritative figure who can show black and white discipline while clearly communicating expectations that hold everyone accountable. This sets a standard for success.

While employees need a disciplinary leader, they also need a loving leader who can also show positive reinforcements when team members work excellently and exceed expectations. But you must be careful not to be overly friendly with your staff. **Very few people can be disciplinary and friendly at the same time, since very few people have learned the art of compartmentalizing.** Learn to compartmentalize, and you will begin to recognize when you need wear the disciplinary hat and when you need to wear the friendly hat.

Chapter 35 - The Unfavorable Position

When I was fighting professionally, I intentionally trained scenarios where I was forced into tough-to-get-out-of positions. I was automatically placed in the losing position and I had to work myself out of the unfavorable position so that I could realistically prepare for future fights.

This training is also necessary for businesses, but must be handled appropriately. This training is called objection handling, which we briefly skimmed over earlier in the book. **If you train your staff to handle objections that may upset the normal flow of things, then they will be better prepared for conflict resolution and the unexpected obstacle when it does occur.** Intentionally training and role-playing with your staff can prepare them for unfavorable scenarios like dealing with an unhappy client or a frustrated business partner.

I love role-playing the following objection with my listing specialist, "I don't want to list my house with you, I want to list it myself. My neighbor just sold their house 'for sale by owner,' so I'm not interested in wasting my money on using a listing agent when I know I can just do it myself." I teach my listing specialist to respond to the client in a way that listens to what they have said. **The agent will affirm the client and ask questions, but also direct the conversation in a way that gives my agent a chance to serve the client.**

Since we hold such a high belief in ourselves and our product and since we pride ourselves in serving our clients with top notch service to attain the best results for them, we do not want to walk away from an opportunity that could best serve a client. **Your team needs to know your core values, beliefs, and systems so that each team member is prepared to explain why your business is the**

best and first of its kind. Believe that you are the only one who can offer the client the best deal.

Teach your team how to overcome their limiting belief or lack of ambition to handle a challenge when it knocks on the door. Fear is a liar! Train your staff to listen well to the client and affirm them. Maintain etiquette in conversation and speak politely to everyone. Handle objections with skill and attain what is best for the client. Help the client understand how and why you will help them better than anyone else will. **You teach your team how to sell your service when you teach them how to wisely handle objections.**

Another aspect to training in "unfavorable positions" is the need to train with an experienced partner. When I trained unfavorable fighting scenarios, if I trained with inexperienced fighters who didn't challenge me in the ways I needed to be challenged, then I didn't learn. I became lazy with poor training and got used to implementing inferior technique. Even though I had lots of training experience with unfavorable positions, some of it was poor experience because of the level of the training partner I had. I did not always have someone in the gym with the experience of the opponent I would be fighting in the cage...so not all the training experience I had was profitable experience. I should have been training those unfavorable positions with people at my level or higher, experts at that specific discipline and technique.

All experience is not income producing experience, and poor training is a waste of time. Do not let your team spend their time inefficiently. Team members may be wasting their time by role-playing situations with other team members who may not have the experience needed in objection handling, or who may distract them with off-topic conversations that derail income producing activities. Their inefficient training can also stem from non-realistic simulations or required classes that do not contain information pertinent to each team member's time or skills. **Do not waste your**

team's precious time with inefficient training techniques or experience that your team doesn't need.

As you may know, one of the most important parts of hiring process is looking for someone with experience. However, even if it looks good on a resume, not all experience is good experience. **If the potential new hire has been trained by someone with less experience who kept a poor work ethic, then their experience would be a negative addition to your team.** You cannot settle for mediocrity or less than the best on your team. You must carefully assess the type of experience a potential hire may have. **Make sure your team members are trained with the level of experience you require for your business to run most efficiently to become a scalable and sell-able business.**

Chapter 36 - Steam is Hotter Than the Boil

A house purchase is the biggest buying or selling process that any client will ever experience. This house purchase may be the client's only transaction like this in their entire lifetime. Clients can quickly become stressed and so emotionally involved that they expect their real estate agent to become their personal counselor. I teach my real estate team to realize that clients have the right to think this way since it is their only transaction happening at that time and it is a big deal to them. **Recognizing that clients' feelings are valid enables your team to serve the customer and meet their needs**.

Business people are not salespeople. Business people are truly customer service people who may not realize that they are customer service people.

A business or a team must realize that the customer is always right. The customer's feelings must always be validated, whether the customer is right or wrong. The truth is that the client feels the way they do for a reason, and the business needs to make the proper accommodations to ensure that the client receives the best service, and more importantly, that they *feel* like they're receiving the best service.

You and your team were hired to do a job that essentially serves your clients and fellow service providers. So the outside perspective of the client or business partner is what really matters since that perspective is what can either help or harm your business. If you have done anything throughout the transaction process that would make your client feel like they did not 100% receive satisfactory service from your business, then they will tell the whole world how terrible their experience was. This will spread like wildfire. When the situation begins to boil over, it will only get worse if you do not work to contain the situation and help the client understand that their perspective is validated.

The client's feelings are right, whether they are right or wrong to you, their feelings are what they feel, and they are led to think or feel that way for a reason. **Find out what that reason is and work to provide them with only good reasons to thank your business and not harm your business.**

It is always better to over communicate with clients rather than under communicate with clients. Over communication is vital to the entire business, especially in resolving a situation with an unsatisfied customer. No one ever complains about receiving over-communication, they only complain when they believe they have received too little communication or service.

Think of a filled-to-the-brim pot about to boil over, with billows of steam curling from the pot into the air. It's hard enough to keep the pot from boiling over, but the vaporized steam from the boil is even hotter than the water in the pot. If your hand gets too close to the steam for too long, then the burn from the steam will hurt more severely than the burn from the water.

The same is true with unsatisfactory clients in a business situation gone awry. **You want to keep the situation from boiling over if you can, while realizing that the steam coiling from the situation will be even hotter than the boil itself if not contained properly.** The steam that rises from the situation will hurt your business even more than the situation itself because of the bad reviews and bad reputation to follow. This burn will lose clients and be severely detrimental to your future business.

Handle situations from a level of high service and excellent communication from the beginning of the relationship or transaction.

If your business truly did provide poor communication or service, then make up for it. **You and your team members were hired to make sure the business proves successful in its business relations and transactions. If a transaction or conversation does end poorly, then take full responsibility and apologize to the client or business partner.** Be the bigger business and in humility, make it right. Provide an even higher level of service to make it right. One upset client will tell fifty people about their experience with your business, and one happy client will tell three people. Understand how detrimental your upset clients will be to your business if you neglect to make up for their poor experience. **Always be careful to keep your clients satisfied and serve them from a high level of service.**

Chapter 37 - The Hand That Feeds You

A fighter never succeeds because of his own brute strength. He needs a support system and training regiment to help him succeed. He needs coaches to hold him accountable and push him farther than he can push himself, and he understands that he must treat these people well if he wants to continue receiving their services.

My dad used to tell me, "Don't mess with anyone who handles your money, your food, or knows the law." Although this is a good rule of thumb, these people do take care of us, and in turn should be well taken care of by us. It is important that we, in both our lives and businesses, take care of the people who take care of us.

If your business receives a referral from a client, send the client a bottle of wine or a gift card to their favorite restaurant as a "thank you." If your business has a profitable month, give 50% of the profits away to help the community, police officers, medical personal, military, firefighters, school teachers, animal shelters, nursing homes, or rehabilitation centers. When you eat out at a restaurant, give a 75% tip to the young server as a "thank you" for helping you. You never know what may be happening in someone else's life, so take the step out of your own world to help another soul.

Choose to put someone else's needs before your own and you'll never know the impact that it may have on them. There are people out there who need more than you do. Are you so small minded to believe that you are the only person in the world who needs to be well provided for?

If you aim for success in your own life then you must first aim to make a difference in someone else's life. Do not set big

goals if you do not have big actions or a big heart. Turn off your pride and turn up your generosity.

If the community takes care of your business by providing you with business or providing for your personal needs, pay them back. Give back to the community to thank them for their business. If your sphere of influence (friends, family, past clients, and acquaintances) provide you with business, make sure they are rewarded. Pay them back for their business to you with an appreciation gift, meal, action, card, or whatever says, "Thank you!" in a language that means the most to them. **Give back to them expecting nothing in return**. Recognize that others may not or cannot return the favor to you. This is when your act of kindness will mean the most.

Your community takes care of you and should be well taken care of by your business. Thank your police officers, firefighters, school teachers, community, animal shelters, past clients, local restaurants, after school cares for kids, elderly, and the list continues. **Thank those who take care of you and your needs, both in business and personally.**

My teams love feeding breakfast to the firefighters, police officers, and teachers on a regular basis. It is so important to care for your community. Do something that no other business around you is doing to say "thank you." Host client appreciation parties for your valued clients.

My Georgia team has rented out a theatre and blocked off the town square to provide a fun movie night to families, with our sponsors providing food and refreshments. My Tennessee real estate team loves throwing client appreciation and community outreach events as well. Remember in anything that your business does, it must always aim to take care of those who take care of it.

Compartmentalize emotions out of your business. Put your needs and wants on the back burner EVERY TIME. When your business gets caught up with clients and what they need, the whole focus of the business changes. Work your hardest to care for your clients, and work even harder to get them out of a deal if it would be best for them to get out of it (even if it means a lost deal for you).

Thank them well. Show them you care, do not just tell them. If you cannot spend any money to express your appreciation, spend your time. In my case and probably yours, community is the reason we are all able to succeed in our goals since we work with the community, we build the team through the community, we change their lives as we grow, and we help them in business.

We are never our own reason for our success. If you think for one second that you are the reason behind your own success, get ready to destroy your business with your prideful and selfish mindset. It is never about yourself. Success is achieved because others have helped you, you cannot and will never be able to succeed solely on your own.

I remember as a kid that there was someone who was always generous to me and my family. As I grew older, there was always someone at dinners who bought the whole table dinner and it blew my mind that they could do that without worrying about money. The level of their generosity stood out to me. When you give back to others and show them your appreciation, you are showing them gracious and generous acts that they'll remember.

From a young age I always wanted to be that generous guy. My goal was to be able to sit down with any number of my friends at any restaurant and let them order whatever they wanted to without them worrying about paying the check. It is so important to give back to those who have helped, supported, and loved you. **You are** where are you now because of the people who help you get here. Take a moment to thank them because no one reaches goals alone.

Chapter 38 - Reaching the Summit

If you've ever watched professional fights or been in the fighting world yourself, you know that each fighter has a "cornerman." Each cornerman encourages their fighter through thick and thin and has the highest amount of influence on their fighter when he is in the ring. No fighter chooses a cornerman who will discourage them or negatively influence them in a fight. A cornerman is on the same team as the fighter and helps that fighter win. That cornerman helps the fighter climb to the top of their mountain.

After a big win, my coaches and I celebrated everyone's hard work. Everyone played a part in obtaining the win, so everyone celebrated together.

I want to succeed, like many people do, but I want to be surrounded by those who want to succeed as well. I don't want to be around people who settle for mediocrity or half-ass a job and give up easily. I want self-motivated people to challenge me and other team members to succeed beyond farther limits than we could ever imagine.

After climbing a high mountain, I want to be surrounded by people that I have climbed with or helped climb up to the mountaintop, I would never want to sit at the top by myself with no one around me to support me or celebrate the win. But I also don't want to pull others up to the top of the mountain by my own strength. I need people climbing with me who will also help each other climb. I need people who will climb with blood, sweat, and tears until they get to the top and then want to keep climbing.

Your business needs to have a team of cornermen on staff who are in it to win it for the long-run. Not only does a business need a strong team who is self-motivated to climb high mountains and help each other keep climbing, but each business needs to recognize those along the way who have helped the business grow and stay on course. **Everyone and every business has someone who has helped them with advice, coaching, finances, and everything else along the way to success**. We all have our lists of cornermen who have helped us climb the highest of mountains. We best not forget any one of them.

I was a mean and rough kid because of the people I hung around, but my childhood best friend was always a good kid and saw the best in me. Cliff Mahala. Cliff kept me pointed in the right direction no matter what kind of trouble I got myself into. In fact, he is the one who encouraged me to participate in the organized sport of fighting. He helped me gain control and highly influenced my path for the better. He was a cornerman who helped direct my course to the right mountain in life and rooted for me even in the losses.

The worst type of person is the person who succeeds but forgets how they achieved their success and who helped them achieve it. As a leader you must remember who has helped you in your success. **You must teach your team to remember those and thank those who have helped them in their success**. When you help people climb up the mountain, get people up there who won't forget how they got there or who helped them achieve their success.

As for choosing your cornermen, remember that people are scared, intimidated, or upset by things they do not understand. Anyone who tells you anything negative cannot see what you see. **You need to surround yourself by people who can help you get to the next level - people who see and share your vision.** Quit hanging out with negative people who will not help you get to the next level or keep cheering you on when you face a challenge. Even if they are your own family - get them out of your life. This may sound harsh, but **removing this negativity will be helpful in ways**

you may not understand until you do it. Find people who will reach down, give you their hand, and help you up to the top of the mountain so that you can keep helping others up.

When you quit climbing you quit helping. Surround yourself with other climbers, not quitters. Find your own cornermen and thank those who have helped you get to where you are now.

Chapter 39 - Stay Great

If I could choose to be any superhero, I would most definitely be Thor. A bad-ass who does not put up with any bullshit. Although Superman is great, he automatically becomes less great when he meets Thor, a hero without the weakness of kryptonite. You may disagree with me and that's fine. If you think a grizzly bear is the greatest of all bears, he automatically becomes less great when he meets a Pizzly or Grolar bear (yes, they exist), which is a hybrid of the polar bear and grizzly bear.

Good is great until good meets great. Then good is only good, not great. If you think you are the best in the business, you are wrong. There is always someone greater. **Your job is to find that someone who is greater. Then compete with greater until you become even better.** Whether your business owns the market or the competition for your business seems to be non-existent, do not worry. The competition is coming. And when it comes you will forfeit if you're not ready to compete. If you are not already sweating, you will be. Anticipate the challenge and start fighting now for the win.

I remember training at my home gym where everyone knew my weaknesses and I knew everyone else's. Even though they knew my weaknesses, I had a psychological advantage above most of them since I was stronger and more aggressive than most of them. That made me great in that room. Once my training was leveled up, I found myself in bigger rooms filled with higher level athletes. Although I was a great fighter in the small room, I realized that I was only a decent fighter in the bigger room. **You must put yourself in other rooms filled with higher competition in order to keep leveling up.**

In real estate, you can be the best single agent in your market center or brokerage but when you compare to a higher market center or better team, then the competition will always be better than you. Every time.

The higher the competition, the higher the cream will rise to the top. Are you disciplined enough to find the higher competition and challenge your business to rise to the occasion and fight for the win?

You and your business are only as good as your competition. You can be great in one setting with little competition, but when your competition becomes greater than your business, then your business will no longer be great and will be forgotten.

The better your business's competition means the better you will push yourself and your business to become. Good is "great" until good meets GREAT. Do you want to be known as a good business, or the BEST one in the market? Don't let your "good" business become "subpar" because of unprepared and undisciplined strategies to compete with greater businesses. Stay ahead of the game. Keep aiming for the growth and expansion of the business, while staying consistent in your procedures and practices, and doing what no one else in the market wants to do or will do. When you meet your goals, keep competing against yourself. If you **stay GREAT and compete with greater so that you and your business can be challenged and continue to grow, then you'll stay at the top of your marketplace and keep reaching new levels of success.**

If you settle for being the "greatest" then you will soon find your business in second place. Third place. Fourth place. But if you stay in competition with yourselves and greater businesses in your field, then your business will be on track to becoming the best that it can be.

Chapter 40 - Partnership to Ownership

I have witnessed many Mixed Martial Arts gyms turn into unsuccessful gyms because of terrible multiple ownership partner situations. Some owners decide to partner with each other because they are scared and do not want to enter the business alone. They want someone else's opinion to affirm their own and share the blame or victory. They don't partner for the right reasons, so their businesses are apt to fail. These owners want companionship and do not have the confidence in themselves to succeed without companionship. They do not have the will-power or courage to step into something new by themselves until they find the right people to help them.

When they rush into a partnership just because they want to start something quickly, they make mistakes and may become partners with someone who they cannot cooperate with well.

Essentially, there are two types of people, Visionaries and Integrators. You can deny the system but at the end of the day we all fit into this pattern one way or another. Like clockwork. When owners pair together, they both risk many resources, time, and money in the partnership as they build the foundation of the business together. Both types of people will experience their own risks and losses besides the source of income or salary that they face when they partner with someone in business. Partnerships require compromises to be made and risks to be taken. The book *Rocket Fuel* by Gino Wickman and Mark Winters explains the right type of partnership in detail.

You don't need to partner with someone if you're not at a high enough risk to lose money, resources, or time. Or else you may not be properly motivated and will fail to pull your weight in the new business partnership. If you have a strong source of income flowing in from another business that you are working in but you want to start another new business, then you are most likely NOT at a high enough risk to start a partnership business unless you decide to invest a major portion of your money, resources, and time into the new business. If you have invested something greater than just your income and will lose a great amount of money, resources, and time if the new business goes south, then you do need a visionary-integrator duo partnership and will do well in that partnership.

Unless you are greatly motivated, you will not work to the level of capacity that you should be working if you start a business partnership with someone who isn't serious enough about the vision or strong enough to complement your weaknesses.

To match well the visionary-integrator duo, the integrator must be detail-oriented and see the smaller picture to help build the business to a high level. The visionary needs to be big-picture oriented and create big ideas for growth, business, and the team to continue expanding so that the integrator can continue implementing.

You should not partner with someone in business simply because you do not want to be in it alone. That excuse is cowardly. Partner with someone if you have poured blood, sweat, tears, money, time, resources, and more into a business or team that you do not want to see turn upside down. **Partner with someone who agrees with your core values but is opposite in personality type.** Not so opposite that you clash on every decision, but different enough to boost each other's business and discipline.

Your partner needs to have something that you do not. **Everyone wants to partner with someone with lots of money thinking that it will help their business succeed. But truly that is**

not how businesses succeed. Money is a band-aid on a puncture wound, but you will need stitches that help the deep wound heal.

Teams that pair with visionaries and integrators succeed because there is a common goal and each person can exercise their strengths and gifts within this partnership. **Partner with someone who can be a gamechanger in the business and bring value that you cannot**. When you partner together, start at the bottom and develop the systems and procedures as you grow so that you are constantly learning to be more efficient. This partnership may take some adjustment, but when you get into the grove with each other then this bond will be unbreakable. So be wise in building your partnership, and when it is built, be careful to protect who joins the team.

Chapter 41 - Old Dogs Must Learn New Tricks

Old dogs can be more stubborn than most, just like old men may be more stubborn than most younger men, because they don't need anyone's approval or opinion. Even if an opinion given to an elderly man is constructive, or a new trick will be rewarding for an old dog to learn, chances are that neither will be well accepted.

Toward the end of my fighting career, I noticed that new fighters came into the sport every day. Even now I constantly hear of new up and coming fighters who never existed when I was professionally competing. Older fighters have been forced to learn new techniques and skills to stay in the game. Some younger fighters are discovering new techniques that have never been used before, and older fighters are fools if they disregard the new skills. The old dog must learn new tricks if he even wants a chance to win the prize against the underdog.

Many fighters who I trained are now black belts in Jiu Jitsu and other arts, and are competing on very high levels. At one time I coached them, but they have far surpassed my training and are now coaching me. The fight game is continuously evolving at a high level. Trainers and nutritionists are constantly researching new philosophies for more efficient training and diet plans. There are new defense strategies discovered for a new fighting position, or a better escape from a submission.

When you think you are too good to learn, your business dies. There are mega-businesses in the world that have suffered horribly because they have refused to stay with the times and learn the new tricks. Many of the well-known businesses that were around when I was growing up are gone because they were replaced by newer, more technologically advanced businesses.

Technology not only makes business easier, but it also replaces the workforce in some cases since it allows businesses to leverage themselves. If your business **embraces technology and learns to leverage it appropriately, it will lead to the further success and growth of the business.** The minute you think your business cannot benefit from the latest discovery, or that you are too experienced to listen to advice of the rookie-business of the year, your business will crumble.

Like I mentioned in a previous chapter, **everyone has something to offer you if you open your ears to listen.** Remember, since the consumer mindset is what matters, so if the consumer thinks your product is faulty in an area, listen to them. They know what they are talking about. They may even know more about an aspect of your product than you do. Ask how your business can improve or resolve that issue.

Even someone with lack of knowledge, experience, and expertise can help your business in some way. **Learning how to leverage the new constructive opinions of an ever changing generation and accept the technological advances of an advancing age will allow exponential growth for your business.** Your business will continue to improve and stay with the times as it learns the "new tricks" to stay ahead of the other businesses.

You must continually put your pride aside and learn to utilize the newest "trick" or technological advance. Shut your mouth and turn down your pride so that you can listen to the inexperienced customer or new team member who may have an excellent idea to offer. Everyone will contribute something to your business if you let them. This is how your business will continue to learn new lessons and tricks to stay on the cutting edge of the market.

Chapter 42 - Medium 5

There's good kid who has started coming to my kickboxing gym to train. One evening I saw a group of five hooligans coming to pick him up after training and I could sense trouble from a mile away. Before he went outside to meet them I pulled him aside and asked, "What do those guys out there look like to you – do they look successful or do they look like thugs?" He knew the answer. I continued, "Where do you see yourself in five years if you keep hanging out with them?" I didn't need to say anything more, he understood, and I never saw him hanging out with those guys again.

You are the happy medium of the five people you spend the most time with. If you surround yourself with negative people, you will become a negative person. If you surround yourself with positive people, you will become a positive person. If you surround yourself with people who hold to good morals, you'll find yourself holding to good morals. If you rank as the alpha male or alpha female among your friends, or find yourself continuously discouraged by your friends, then you need to find new friends. Your friends need to challenge you but not idolize you. Your friends need to offer constructive criticism when necessary, but not humiliate you.

Let's say you are climbing a tall ladder. If you are at the bottom of the ladder, then you're always reaching up to get to the next rung or grabbing a hold of someone's hand above you. This also means that someone else is always reaching down to help you climb. This gets old.

If you're climbing a ladder but solely depending on other people to help you climb, then you may not be adding value to those on the ladder with you. If you find yourself at the very top of the ladder, then you have a whole slew of people to help off the ladder when they reach the top with you. If you're always reaching down, then you're never being challenged to keep climbing another ladder or receive help from others.

But if you find yourself in the middle of the ladder, however, then you are able to help some people climb up with you while also receiving help from others above you, and continuing to climb yourself. This is a happy medium.

In business, you need people who can help you move up the ladder while you are also helping others at different levels of business climb their ladder.

When you start working your way up to the top of the ladder, you need to make new networks of new people who can challenge you in new ways. Like I mentioned earlier, be the hardest worker in the room, and when you have become the hardest worker in one room it is time to find a new one. **Climb the ladder until you near the top, then find a new ladder to climb with new challenges and people to surround you as you climb.**

Get rid of the negative influences in your life that are keeping you from reaching your full potential.

If you are married to an abusive husband, get divorced. If you are best friends with a "negative Nancy" who complains about everything, get a new best friend. If you are in a work environment that does not value your level of expertise or refuses to respect your worth, quit and find a better job. It sounds easy, but in reality this will be difficult. If it were easy then people would actually do it. Soon enough you'll realize how these negative influences are poorly affecting your work and personal life. **So, take the leap of faith and start surrounding yourself with good, positive, healthy mindsets that will challenge you in greater discipline to achieve your goals.** Weed out everyone else, they don't matter. You are not obligated to them, so rid yourself of their influence and you will thank me a year from now. Then surround yourself with people that will hold you accountable to the discipline that you need in your life.

Chapter 43 - Being Your Best

When I first started my fighting career, I had an excellent boxing coach and terrific Jiu Jitsu coach. But I lacked a good kickboxing, strength, and wrestling coach. I had to seek out these specialists to improve my game. So I found kickboxing coaches, wrestling coaches, and strength and conditioning coaches who all helped me build a better game and strategy.

Learn to strengthen your weak points and you will become ten times stronger in the end. If you truly want to become successful, then you will spend more time now sharpening your sword and training harder for the win.

I have mentioned throughout this book that you are not the best in your market center or business, and you will never be the best. No matter how good you think you are, there will always be someone else better than you. Knowing that there is someone better and using that person to motivate you to train harder, fight better, and win is the most helpful thing you can ever do for your own self-growth. The moment you start thinking that you are the best, you stop learning and your motivation to win begins to decrease. **As we talked about earlier, after you have climbed to the top of one ladder, you are still at the bottom of another.**

Do not get a haughty mindset. The Bible even tells us that pride comes before the fall, so once you start puffing with pride your business will start failing. This should not discourage you, but rather encourage you to seek out the best in your business and learn from them. They will challenge your current infrastructure and systems to reach higher levels of success. **Expand your business if you have found that your business is reaching the top of its ladder.** Open another location. Start another business. Start coaching and speaking across the country to teach and challenge others. Think outside the box and you will continue reaching new levels of productivity and success that no one ever thought were possible.

No matter how good you are at executing your business, leading your team, or implementing new tactics, your weak points will always be exposed. **Always strive to improve your weak points and focus on making your strong points stronger. Seek out the right coaches to help you improve your game.**

You improve your game and strategies when you find the right people to train you appropriately to accomplish your goals. If you have not sat down recently to assess your strengths and weaknesses, do it now. Have a close friend of yours interview five people in your office anonymously to tell them what they think your strengths and weaknesses are. You may not be growing in your business or personal life right now because you do not know what you need to focus on in order to see growth. So figure it out. Then focus on growing in those areas.

Learn about the subjects where you are weak or hire someone who is a specialist in those subjects to train you well so that you can become strong. Whether or not you can afford a coach to train you in all your weak areas depends on your leverage. If you lack the finances to hire a specialist, then spend more of your time self-educating yourself in the subjects where you are weak so that you can become stronger. Learn. If you have the money, then hire someone so that they can share their expertise with you.

You do not want the win badly enough if you do not dedicate the time now to forward your growth and become stronger to fight better for the win. If you lack the drive or humility to focus on self-growth, or if you think that you do not need to improve your game, the you might as well give up. And you know how much I hate it when people give up. You should cut your losses now if you don't have the ambition you need to fight hard enough for the win. You're just wasting your time and everyone else's if you keep complaining that you cannot breakthrough to the next level, since you can. You just don't want it badly enough if you refuse to put all the effort forth in improving your weaknesses and increasing your discipline to train well.

So take the steps to find the coach you need to challenge you. **Implement the habits and consistent schedule you need to remain highly disciplined and accountable.** Seek out the best in the business and see what they can teach you. Then shut up, listen, and learn.

Chapter 44 - Roll with the Punches

If coffee spills on a nice shirt at work and no back-up shirt is available, the world does not stop revolving around the sun and life goes on just fine. It may be embarrassing or uncomfortable, but everything will be just fine. There are some things in this world that cannot be controlled. The feeling of a last-minute change of plans is sometimes just plain awful, but in the end, everything works out just fine to adapt well around the change.

People can choose to react with anger, frustration, or a negative attitude to any of these examples which only makes the situation worse since nothing can be done. Why worry or become angry when nothing can be done? It is a waste of energy and only heightens a situation that at the end of the day, simply "is what it is." If life goes on, we should too, and save our anger and frustration for another time more worthy of it.

In the art of Boxing and other Mixed Martial Arts, if an opponent gets hit but tries to stiff-jaw and take the punch, then the punch will be far more effective than if the opponent were to simply go limp and roll with the punch, letting the punch move him. **Instead of trying to be a strong immovable rock, everyone in the fight world knows that rolling with the punches is a much more effective defense than trying to tough out the punch.**

This ideology correlates so well in business. **When a negative situation or conflict hits your business head on, do not dig your feet into the ground or you will get beat up. Roll with the punches.** Life will go on. The world will not end. Do not worry yourself sick and incorrectly exert the energy you that you need adapt well to the situation. When there is a shift in the real estate market or a dip in your market for the business, adapt. Change your procedures to handle the shift or conflict. **Adapt your fighting** strategy and then fight back and move forward when you stabilize. **Do not exhaust your business by trying to constantly flex up to take the punches, roll with them.** Change to conquer. If you cannot adapt then you cannot succeed.

Practice adapting appropriately to unwelcome changes or situations in your personal life and it will become natural to adapt to misfortune in your business life. Remember, revert to the worst-case scenario plan that you should have made before the situation presents itself. If you cannot control the situation before it arises, take a deep breath to regain your composure. Think positively from the 30,000-foot aerial view of the situation and ask questions to find a solution or adaptation to the issue. If nothing can be done, then do not exhaust yourself worrying about it. Go around the roadblock and keep pushing for the win. Roll with the punches.

An oak tree that may look strong has no flexibility against the forceful wind and will snap, but bamboo is flexible against the wind and bends in reaction to the wind's force. Be flexible. Do not be stiff or your business will snap in half under the weight of the opposing force. **Adapt with flexibility, roll with the punches, and fight back when you regain your composure and stability.**

Chapter 45 - Micro-management vs. Macro-management

If your wife or mother tells you to clean up a mess, they simply tell you to clean up the mess. They don't tell you to use the green dustpan, with the red broom, the specific plant-based non-toxic housecleaner with the specific micro-fiber mop and instruct you through each step of the process. (Well, maybe in your case they do, but for this example let's pretend they don't.) There's not an operations manual that walks you through the process step-by-step. If you and your spouse decide to take a twelve-hour road trip and your spouse is driving, then let them drive. Don't back-seat drive and micro-manage them for twelve hours, or else you'll get kicked out of the car and end the road trip early with a possible divorce. If a boss asks his employee to submit a ten-page report analyzing market trends and correlations, he should not hover over the employee offering suggestions for every sentence until the employee is finished writing.

This is the difference between macro-managing and micro-managing. **The objective with macro-managing is to point someone in the right direction but not lead them on a strict leash through every step.**

I have seen too many business leaders lose staff members because of their desire to control every detail of everything. Even down to the detail of how paperwork needs to be stapled. If any leader in your business or team is so controlling that they cannot get over the smallest of details to see what is important, they do not need to be in a leadership position.

A good coach points a good fighter in the right direction without having to provide them with a 10-step process that they micro-manage.

Your objective is to point your staff in a direction within certain parameters, and their job is to complete the task within those certain parameters to reach the objective. **Macro-managing your staff enables them to take leadership and show initiative.** This allows you to use less of your energy directing people *how* to complete the specific task, and enables THEM to use THEIR own creativity to accomplish the task. **When they complete the task their way, they take ownership.** The more ownership they have in their position, the more confident they will be in their ability to succeed and help the business accomplish its goals.

If you find yourself in a position where you're constantly micro-managing any staff member then you've made an incorrect hire for that position (unless it is an entry level position where micro-management is somewhat appropriate). Your hires should know exactly what their responsibilities are and how to complete them. So do not waste your precious time directing them when you do not have to. **This shows them that you don't trust them, or don't have the confidence in them to complete the task well.**

The more you micro-manage, the less your employees will feel motivated to work for you. If you lead supervisors, then coach your supervisors to macro-manage their staff as well.

Your staff will begin to personalize tasks and demonstrate leadership. **Your staff will take ownership when you macro-manage, but your staff will take offense when you micro-manage.** Your business and productivity will reflect whether its leadership micro-manages or macro-manages. Choose wisely and act accordingly for the benefit of everyone else and the business.

Chapter 46 - Time Is a Commodity

As a fighter makes every minute matter leading up to a fight, businesses should also train their team to count every minute towards the win. What are you doing with the twenty-four hours of your day? Is each hour being used to its full potential?

What is your time worth? If you do not know the answer to this then you are not working most efficiently for your business. Take a minute right now to figure out what an hour of your time is worth by calculating your actual hourly rate. Take your yearly pay and divide that by 2,080 (based on a forty-hour work week, multiplied by fifty-two weeks of the year, including no vacation time). This will help you figure out what your dollar per hour pay breaks down to based on your yearly salary. Now that you have this number, first understand that your time is priceless. **No matter what amount of money you currently make, your time is priceless.** Are you treating every second, minute, and hour of your time as priceless?

Second, let's think about this from a business perspective. **No matter what your business is, every business has key performance indicators (KPI) and income producing activities that determine how effectively the business spends its time toward achieving its goals and ultimate success.**

For the sake of an easy example, let's say that you calculated your hourly pay to be $100. Now you can leverage your time to work on specific income producing activities that are worth your time, and less activities that are worth less than $100 an hour. This allows you more time to negotiate business and focus on the key performance indicators that will forward the business. Spend more time training and coaching staff. This allows you the ability to track numbers and set goals without being distracted by the little monotonous details that are not worth your time. **This will teach you how to spend your time to its highest and best use.**

Paperwork is not a $100 an hour activity but rather a $20 or $15 activity. So do not spend your time doing it if your hourly pay is better spent negotiating business deals or coaching staff. **When the paperwork or other task is delegated to a trained employee who is paid $20 an hour, then the hour spent on that job by that trained employee saves the company $80 just by having the trained employee complete the task instead of you.**

You know that time is the only item you cannot replenish or acquire more of, and you know that you cannot work more than twelve or fourteen-hour days per week. Accept that fact. Stop trying to find more hours in the day to work, and instead start trying to work more efficiently and leverage your time wisely. **In addition to using your time wisely according to your hourly pay, you need to stay away from time thieves in your business.** Never procrastinate and always stay away from people who will steal your time like they're stealing from a bank. Keep boundaries to avoid people from wasting your time, do not allow yourself that loss.

Just like you should save your money and invest it in whatever is important – stocks, bonds or real estate – investing your time is no different. **Spend your time like you would spend your money: wisely.**

Regarding investing money, save your time by paying someone else to manage your investments. Maybe you could buy a rental building and use time to your advantage while someone else pays off your debt overtime on the property. Using time as your friend in your investments, especially in relation to rental property, means that you can make more money over more time while someone else pays off your debt, and that is the best kind of investment to keep in your pocket.

Invest your time and money into the avenues that are of value to you or the business. Invest your time and money in the education that would benefit you and the company. Invest your money to make money for you or the company or in others who can help grow the business and save you more money in the long run. Invest your time in nurturing relationships worth more than money can buy.

Chapter 47 - Risk vs. Reward

As fighters train, they need to caution themselves to keep a very aggressive yet skilled training camp. At four weeks into their training camp from training at a higher level, they may be more susceptible to injuries. If an athlete's training partner does not know how to slow down or control himself, since the athlete is already in a depleting state, the risk is too high than the reward for the athlete to continue in his training. The risk of injury and losing money from the fight is higher than the reward of training at the high level to guarantee the win.

The application to business is simple, yet again. Risk vs. reward. If this scale is not used to weigh every decision that is made for the business, then the business will walk blind into a fight and risk a major loss or injury. Investments, relationships, marketing plans, hiring processes, budgeting, and every other department of the business requires this application.

There are many relationships we can create in our businesses or new applicants that could be hired to help move the business forward, but the risk always needs to be considered before that relationship is built. Is that person trustworthy? What is the known reputation of that person? There are plenty of people who have questionable reputations that you could involve yourself with for a short-term game in your business, but in the long-term game, the risk may be greater than the reward. The risk of a lost or tainted reputation from doing business with untrustworthy businessmen is higher than the reward from doing business with them.

Every relationship you have, you must weigh in the risk vs. the reward scale. During the hiring process you must ask yourself, "even if this person may train and interview well, will this person be loyal to the team and moral code that is upheld in this business?" If the risk of a disloyal or nonconformant new hire is greater than the reward of productivity from them, then it isn't worth hiring that person.

In addition to weighing your business relationships on the risk vs. reward scale, you must also weigh your investments on the risk vs. reward scale. For the sake of an example, let's say that you are considering investing in a real estate rental property. On the risk vs. reward scale you want to ensure that you will be receiving at least a 1% return on your real estate rental investment per month after the investment. So, at a $100,000 investment you want to see a return of at least $1,000 a month. This calculation excludes appreciation value and includes a theoretical fully occupied rental property. Let's say that the rental property was built in 1940 and you see that the reward could be profitable and the potential return on your investment could be high, but there is an old HVAC, old flooring, old plumbing and electrical wiring, and the risk of losing money on so many repairs may be greater than the possible reward of the 1% return on investment.

A new marketing strategy always includes risk of failure and a possible reward of increased business. The "pros" and "cons" must be weighed to assess whether or not a new strategy would lead to a profitable result for the business, or if the risk would outweigh the reward.

Just like athletes must discern how great the risk and reward could be in continuing in their training camps, you as an entrepreneur or businessman must also weigh the risk and reward in business relations, investments, and decisions to guarantee the success and growth of the company.

Chapter 48 - Sharpening the Ax

You may have heard the saying before, "sharpen your ax." Obviously, it is easier to cut trees with a sharp ax than it is to cut trees with a dull one. If a lumberjack has four hours to cut down a yard of trees, he should spend at least three of those hours sharpening his ax. **A dull ax will cause him three times as much work and effort as a sharpened ax would, so if he spends the time preparing well for the task then he will finish the job in good time.** The key here is that preparation is everything. **Remember that a dull knife often leads to more injuries than a sharp knife.**

The same is true in fighting. If a fighter walks into a fight without appropriate preparation or the proper training camp structured to defeat his opponent, then he will lose the fight. The fighter needs to study his opponent's strengths and weaknesses in order to be well suited for a victory. If the fighter neglects to study well his opponent and prepare appropriately, he cannot expect a win and will pay the price for his lack of discipline.

In business, if you walk into a conference room unprepared for a meeting or ill-suited for an interview, then the end-result will reflect your preparation. Your unprepared material will cause you a loss. If your ax would have been sharper, then you most likely would have succeeded instead of failed. Seems simple, yet how many times a day do we forfeit preparation and fail to plan ahead for the win?

Have you ever walked out of your house without your phone, keys, wallet, lunch or glasses? Or left the office in a hurry and forgot an important file that you needed to bring home to finish working on? So many times we fail to think ahead even in the small things and pay the price for them. If we train ourselves to be better prepared in the smaller things, we will naturally train ourselves to be better prepared in the bigger things. Run through a short checklist on your way out of the door in the mornings so that you will not forget the items you need – phone, keys, wallet. Done.

Spend more time in the mornings sharpening your sword. Wake up earlier. Eat a more substantial breakfast. Study harder. Ask yourself harder questions to increase your productivity and preparation. What can you exploit or leverage to your business' advantage to sharpen its ax and become more efficient in the long-run? In what areas can you increase efficiency to better prepare for transactions, projects, or negotiations? What topics can you educate yourself or your team on even more than you are now to lead to further success? Think about these questions for your business as you sit down to sharpen its ax.

It is imperative to spend time sharpening the ax so that your business avoids walking into the woods and realizing the ax is too dull to chop down any trees. This will avoid much pain and long suffering when a deal may fall through due to lack of preparation. **Work to guarantee your team the victory over a difficult opponent and gain the upper hand in any fight.** Educate yourself before walking into a conference room for a meeting. Do your research and know who you are talking to before you talk to them. Do not tackle any task without first educating yourself and preparing yourself adequately for the fight.

I'm currently involved with many business realms that I knew very little of years ago, but with education, teaching resources, many audio books, and a little experience, my ax is sharper than it was when I started. Even if you don't feel confident in an area of study now, you can become a master of it when you determine to sharpen that ax.

Your goal should always be to become the smartest man in any room on any subject you find yourself talking about. **Make** friends who can help you scale up, sharpen your ax, and teach you about a topic that you know little about. Discipline yourself to prepare for a fight before walking into one.

If you are meeting with a high-level financial advisor or investor, know your facts and do your research before the meeting so that you are not walking ignorantly into a transaction. Take the time to sharpen your ax in a topic that you are only pretending to know what you are talking about. Listening to audio books daily will increase your knowledge and confidence in topics that will allow you to transact more successful business. **Ultimately, prepare yourself and your business to work more efficiently and think ahead.** Learn to sharpen the ax before cutting down trees.

Chapter 49 - A Humble and Fearless Leader

You can study the world's greatest leaders and coaches to find commonalities between them all. Leaders and coaches are fearless. They realize that fear is a liar and they refuse to believe fear's lies. Great leaders and coaches are humble. If they're not humble, they're not great. Great leaders build others up before they turn to themselves, and when they become prideful they cease being great. Great coaches are confident. Confident in the mission and vision that they are forwarding, and confident in themselves and their team to carry out the mission and vision. If they are not confident in their belief system, they cannot lead others well in that belief system. Great leaders and coaches are educated. The minute they cease to be a great teacher, they cease being a great leader.

Leaders should be confident, humble, educated, and fearless. The aim is never to be a slave driver, but never a best friend. Never prideful, but never underconfident. Never boastful, but never uneducated.

Team leaders need to make sure that shit gets done. They are pieces on the chess board like everyone else. **Team leaders need to be in the trenches with their team leading correctly.** When they're found in the trenches, leading by example and doing what is expected of their team members better, faster, and more efficiently, they become leaders who can be trusted. If a leader cannot take a spoonful of his own medicine when necessary, he's not great enough to be followed by others.

Some team leaders need to realize that when they are acting as a slave driver, they aren't acting as a leader. **Slave drivers lead by fear and intimidation which is not a long-term motivator.** Slave drivers only motivate people to follow them when those people are bound with chains, paychecks, or when people are driven by pure, desperate necessity. This is not sustainable for a business.

If people can trust and follow you naturally without a leash, then you know that they *want* to rely on your leadership. When you walk into the office and see that the office needs to be swept or the trash needs to be taken out, you do it. When you see that the business is below its prospecting goals for the month and a hundred more calls need to be made, you stay late and make the hundred calls.

Leaders become great when they realize that they are not better than anyone else. The Bible says that the last here on earth shall be first and the first here on earth shall be last in the Kingdom. If self-righteousness is guiding you, it is guiding you down a self-destructive path and you will soon find that no one wants to follow a self-righteous leader. If you are motivated by the desire to help other people succeed and you demonstrate this by word and deed, you will find that many people will want to follow a leader who, out of humility, considers others better than himself.

At the end of the day, it is necessary to recognize that we are all human. We're all on the same playing field. The CEO is just as equal as the janitor in any business. **They are both needed to keep the business running since all game pieces are crucial for the win.** Be humble, confident, educated, and fearless in your leadership and you will see the business soar in productivity, morale, and success.

Chapter 50 - Consistency Wins

I mentioned previously that hard work beats talent every time. In the same way, consistency beats motivation every time. Keeping a consistent diet and exercise regimen (whether or not you feel like it) for one full year is much better than feeling motivated to keep a healthy regimented schedule as a New Year's resolution but failing to do so after the motivation disappears. **If consistency is implemented in any habit or schedule, success is guaranteed**.

Whether or not you like it, you are a creature of habit. You do certain actions in a certain order without even realizing it, as if you're operating on autopilot. You'll establish habits as you remain consistent in doing things you may not want to do. Before long, you may not even realize that you are doing the things you once hated to do (like getting up early to go to the gym), because they have become so engrained in your everyday routine that you could not operate without them.

If you are trying to quit a bad habit, staying consistent in fighting that habit by following your strict, planned out schedule to avoid encountering that habit is guaranteed to break the habit vs. depending on the ever-fleeting "desire" to quit the habit. If you are trying to break the habit of nail biting and every time you "feel" like biting your nails you determine to consistently engage your fingers in an alternative activity, then you consistently train the craving to initiate another action. Every time. This consistent action replaces the previous action and will soon break the habit faster than trying to rely on "feeling" the desire to quit the habit.

Our emotions are not consistent, so if we depend on them to form or break our habits, we will fail every time. We must implement discipline and strengthen our will-power muscle to do what we do not want to do and remain slaves to our schedule even when we don't "feel" like it. **Consistency beats motivation every time.**

Athletes who are consistent in their training schedules (whether or not they feel like it) will be consistent in their success. **Consistency is a systematic approach to winning and is the most important aspect in any sport.**

When a business is consistent in their prospecting, sales, and success, then they also experience more discipline, knowledge and experience. Consistency is key. **Discipline, knowledge, and experience are qualities attained by consistency.** Soon consistency will form autopilot habits that will lead to success.

My business coach, Coach David Keesee, calls people who are not consistent "try babies." These people try something for a week but do not see immediate results, so they quit since their motivation for instant gratification has disappeared. They are the epitome of inconsistency at its finest. **Anything works for as long as you do**.

You could be consistent with a bad idea that should not naturally bring success, but with consistency you will find a way to make it work. If you cannot try a system or a new idea for at least six months before moving on from it, then it isn't worth trying at all.

Certify that your business is consistent with all systems and procedures for six months at least. Then after six months you'll have enough information to step back and properly assess if any of the systems or procedures need to be tweaked in order to optimize efficiency.

If your business is consistent then it will beat out other businesses who fail to be consistent, and surprisingly, this inconsistency applies to almost every real estate team in the business. Real estate agents especially are always trying new marketing strategies and scripts, new processes and checklists, but fail to be consistent in their new endeavors and end up relying on a fleeting motivating morale to drive them forward. This is not sustainable for any business, especially one with a fluctuating market. **Refuse to rely on fleeting motivators to drive your team forward, and be consistent in your systems, procedures, and habits to achieve your goals and success.**

Conclusion

Forge yourself through fire. Forge your business through fire. This is the only way that the old will disappear and the new "you" and new "business" will be formed. Test your discipline in harsher ways than I suggested in this book. Hold each other so strictly accountable in your business that there is no room for any slacking by anyone. Challenge each other. Implement new habits of self-education. Think positively for everything. Avoid quitting at all costs. Get up earlier to exercise more will-power doing things you do not want to do.

This may be uncomfortable, but the end product will be one hundred times better than anything else you can imagine. When business leaders, entrepreneurs, and ambitious people who want to succeed adopt these very simple tactics that work and implement them to everyday life – both at home and at work – they have the power to change their route to success. They can change their expectations. Change their outcomes. Change their mindset. They can serve clients from a higher level of service. They can become more positive, more educated, and more disciplined. They reorient themselves to focus on their ultimate mission, vision, values, and strengths. **They find themselves on the narrow way to success. Anyone can do this. It is so simple! And if anyone can do this, then you can do this. No one is holding you back expect for yourself.** Anyone can be successful in their business. Guaranteed. The only way that you will prove me wrong is if you don't try. Or if you fail to give 100% of effort when you do try.

When consistency and discipline are increased in one area of life, they naturally increase in all areas of life. One step at a time. **Stop believing the lies that you tell yourself every day that are keeping you from great opportunities and costing you**

further success. Stop surrounding yourself with negative influences that will continue to destroy your mindset. **Stop telling yourself that you've hit your limit of success and cannot achieve anymore breakthroughs – or else you will become a slave to that prophesy.** Stop telling yourself that you cannot push yourself any harder to succeed, because you of all people know that you can always work harder.

You can always grow stronger. You just must want it badly enough and truly put forth the effort to do it. **You can be limitless if you let yourself loose** and unlock the potential that you don't think you have. **If you don't implement the discipline and accountability you need to consistently lead to further self-growth in business and personal life, there is someone else who will.** They will take the win from you since you will not take the steps to fight well enough for it.

Implement these fifty tactics and you will succeed. You will become a more positive person and a humbler leader. You will become the person you dreamed of being but thought you could never become. It all starts now. By changing your mindset to change your outcomes.

The effort you input will correlate with the output result. If you only input 50% of your effort to implement these tactics, then you will barely see a 50% return on your investment. If you input 100% of your effort to implement these tactics, then you will see a 100% return on your time, energy, and discipline that will change your life. Don't believe me? Try it. Fight for the win. Fight and train with blood, sweat and tears until you win and become the hardest worker in that gym. Keep climbing new ladders to new successes. You are the only one responsible for changing your mindset, no one else can do this for you. **So own it. Change it. Fight to Win.**